. . . Something made me turn around and look up . . . my heart skipped several beats. Above the rooftop of a small house, an angular craft was descending toward me silently. It was extremely large and a headlight shone down at me. As it glided slowly toward me, at perhaps three or four miles per hour, I froze in terror and awe. . . .

The interior of the craft was completely lit up and I could see everything clearly, including the being sitting in the front seat . . . Its head looked enlarged, bulbous. Its arms and shoulders were broad and very thin.

I bolted down the street and turned to see the craft casually bobbing along next to me . . . I had no way to know its intent. . . .

# SILENT INVASION

## THE SHOCKING DISCOVERIES OF A UFO RESEARCHER

---

## ELLEN CRYSTALL, Ph.D.

St. Martin's Paperbacks

Published by arrangement with Marlowe & Company, an imprint of Avalon Publishing Group

SILENT INVASION

Library of Congress Catalog Card Number: 91-13889

ISBN: 0-312-95935-4

Printed in the United States of America

Paragon House trade paperback and hardcover editions published in 1991
Marlowe & Company trade paperback edition published in 1994
St. Martin's Paperbacks edition/November 1996

St. Martin's Paperbacks are published by St. Martin's Press, 175 Fifth Avenue, New York, NY 10010.

10  9  8  7  6  5  4  3  2

# TABLE OF CONTENTS

ACKNOWLEDGMENTS                                          xi
FOREWORD BY PHILIP IMBROGNO                             xiii
INTRODUCTION                                            xvi

1   IN THE BEGINNING                                       1
2   TOUCHDOWN IN PINE BUSH                                14
3   A PHYSICIST OFFERS HELP                               32
4   CONTACT!                                              39
5   THE INVISIBILITY FACTOR                               46
6   *PM MAGAZINE* GOES INTO THE FIELD                     57
7   OUT OF SIGHT, OUT OF PINE BUSH                        63
8   REENTRY: 1984                                         70
9   ALIENS UNDERGROUND                                    86
10  THE BOOMERANG AND THE BIG ONE                         93
11  MEDIA EXPOSURE AND THE BIRTH OF
    CONTACTEE                                            101
12  ALIEN VIBES                                          107
13  WHERE HAVE ALL THE SAUCERS GONE?
    THE MANY SHAPES OF CRAFT                             112
14  THE HUMAN FACTOR                                     120
15  THE PHOTOGRAPHS—AND ALL UFO
    PHOTOGRAPHS                                          135
16  A DISCUSSION OF SELECTED PHOTOS                      152
17  FRONTIERS OF SCIENCE                                 163

Appendix   EYEWITNESS STATEMENTS                         172

# DEDICATION

I would like to dedicate this book to all
the people who have seen aliens and
crafts and have suffered because of it.

To Harry Lebelson (1937–1995)
You will be missed.

# ACKNOWLEDGMENTS

I almost feel I should thank the elusive and mysterious aliens for causing my obsession, which has led to a lifelong search for answers to many questions about them. When I have all those answers, I'll decide whether the aliens deserved to be thanked. At present, I'm undecided.

Meanwhile, there are hundreds of people who have accompanied me to Pine Bush for research—far too many to name individually. But I collectively thank all who spent time with me. Whether the evenings were fantastically exciting or dull beyond boredom, I'm grateful for their support.

Many residents of Pine Bush played important roles in this project, including some who were abducted by aliens and had terrifying experiences. To all of them, I offer my thanks for tolerating my presence when it sometimes made things difficult and painful because of the emotional depth and power in the UFO experience.

A number of my friends have been regulars at Pine Bush over the years. They have supported me emotionally, given me publicity, and in general acted on my behalf. I offer a heartfelt thank you to Eleanor Motichka, Cathy McCartney, Rick Rohrman, the Schapper family, Cindy Golas, and the Metaphysical Center of New Jersey.

Robert Toto passed away in March, 1990. Bob lived next to Pine Bush. We met in 1986 and had some incredible sightings together. He played a key role in bringing people to Pine Bush. To his wife and daughter, I say thank you.

There are some to whom I'm especially grateful and who deserve special mention. Harry Lebelson, who was UFO editor at *Omni* magazine in 1980, first took me into Pine Bush. Sam Stecher, a physicist who worked with us during the early days of this field study, likewise deserves acknowledgment.

I also extend deep thanks to John White for his perseverance with the project until we got my story into print, and to my publisher for believing in it.

My parents, Beverley and Jesse Crystall, and my two sisters, Sandy and Lisa, have seen UFOs on occasions ranging from distant viewing to close encounters. Although they never chased the ships as I have, they nevertheless hoped that my quest would lead me to the truth about UFOs.

Last in line, but not in the depth of my feeling, I thank David De Lia, who sought me out for Pine Bush excursions after seeing me on television. Although he began by thinking only of the UFO phenomenon, our friendship grew into encouragement, support, and devotion. For that alone, whatever else happens, I may end up thanking the aliens.

# FOREWORD

Since 1982, thousands of people have sighted UFOs in the Hudson Valley of New York. These sightings range from strange lights in the night sky to close encounters in which witnesses got within one hundred feet of an object reported to have been metallic and the size of a football field. The sightings are documented in my book *Night Siege: The Hudson Valley UFO Sightings*, coauthored with Dr. J. Allen Hynek and Bob Pratt. Ellen Crystall's field research was carried out in the Pine Bush area of New York, which is located in the Hudson Valley and is very close to the center of this UFO activity.

One of the greatest problems investigators face when dealing with the UFO phenomenon is the accuracy of what witnesses say happened. Their descriptions are subject to misperception and bias; their memories are fallible; their honesty may be suspect; their motives may be self-serving.

The UFO investigators themselves may be suspect: Are they reporting their case truthfully? Are their data open to inspection? Have they followed the protocols for empirical, objective investigation? Have they properly documented their findings? Have they submitted them for peer review? Have they established the credibility of their conclusions, no matter how incredible the subject under investigation?

This foreword is primarily a tribute to an outstanding UFO researcher and fact finder. I know of none who is more dedicated, trustworthy, and persevering than Ellen

Crystall. Her work documenting UFO phenomena at Pine Bush was done in the field, meticulously collecting the evidence and gathering statements from witnesses. The result of her work, *Silent Invasion*, is an important contribution to ufological reserach.

The UFO phenomenon, increasingly, is coming to the attention of scientists, engineers, and other technically trained people. It is very important that researchers involved document their findings accurately. I feel that Ellen Crystall has done this well. At first, I was somewhat skeptical of the content of *Silent Invasion*, but as I read her manuscript, I found that a great deal of her research paralleled my own. We are both tracking the same elusive phenomenon in the Hudson Valley. To some, the incidents she reports may sound like science fiction, but I can affirm from my own independent investigation of UFO sightings there that the UFO activity in and around Pine Bush is real.

Ellen Crystall calls for and demonstrates through her own experience as a UFO investigator the extreme value of paying attention to the many puzzling UFO reports that have taken place in the Hudson Valley. I feel that this activity has already been recognized in some high places in our government, but certainly not publicly. I leave you to ponder the issue. But about the existence of the UFO phenomenon at Pine Bush, New York, there seems to be little question. So many people from doctors and lawyers, police officers and scientists, to solid citizens from many walks of life, have had strange encounters there with something they considered not of this world that the phenomenon cannot be denied and should not be ignored.

It is my feeling that the work of Ellen Crystall and her colleagues will come to be recognized as a solid contribution to our knowledge of the UFO experience and a clear call for recognizing publicly the scope of the challenge it represents.

Philip Imbrogno, M.S.
Chairman, Science Department
Windward School, White Plains,
New York
Director, The Bowman Observatory
Greenwich, Connecticut

# INTRODUCTION

**THE SINGLE MOST** important event in the history of the human race would be contact with extraterrestrials. Think about that. While the discovery of fire, the invention of language, numbers, and the wheel are undeniably significant in the millennia-long rise of civilization, those events only bring us nearer to the central question of life—they don't answer it. Among everything that occurs on earth every day, the event that would most profoundly change our view of reality and answer our overwhelming search for meaning would be contact with ETs. That would let us know exactly what and who we are in the cosmos.

*That contact has already occurred,* although many people don't believe this to be the case. There are aliens on our planet; they have arrived in UFOs. Millions of people all over the world have seen spaceships. Although thousands have been reported, most sightings go unreported, investigators have found. Moreover, hundreds, perhaps thousands, of people have had direct contact with the aliens. Most contacts still go unreported also, mainly because the experiences are so extraordinary and stressful that they leave people confused and upset, to put it mildly. They challenge our everyday assumptions about reality.

This book is about my direct observations of aliens and their ships—UFOs—and my quest for answers to questions about them: not only the usual "who, what, when, where" but also the "why." I am seeking to discover why I and others have been targeted by aliens for exposure and access to them and their spacecraft. I have some answers. I have new evidence—specifically, photographic data. Based on my personal experiences, research, analysis, and deductive reasoning, the conclusions I've come to—conclusions with which my colleagues agree—are staggering in their implications. One discovery is that there are concentrated landing areas where UFOs almost always can be found, but not everyone who goes to such locations sees UFOs.

In the most general way, everyone involved in UFO contact has his or her special part to play in some field or area of experience, ranging from media exposure to technical expertise, from provision of special equipment to just plain tender loving care for others in this often lonely, bizarre, and frustrating investigation. The search for truth is extremely difficult, but when the rewards come, they are staggering for the questing mind. One of my most fervent wishes is to have what I and other contactees have seen become commonplace for everyone. The ships and their lighting systems, for example, are aesthetically magnificent. When seen even once, they leave no doubt that they are definitely a form of advanced technology—not a figment of anyone's imagination—and that they are part of a supertechnological civilization.

While I and others have watched UFOs, we have been known on occasion to shout questions at them, such as, "Why don't you show yourself to others who don't believe you exist?" and "Why are you revealing your beautiful craft to so few of us?" And most important of all, "Why are you doing this to me?"

My interactions with UFOs thus far can be divided into three periods:

1. Hollywood, California in 1971. This lasted nearly four months.
2. Pine Bush/Crawford, New York, in 1980. Again, this lasted about four months.
3. Pine Bush/Crawford and Middletown, New York, from 1984 until the present.

Each episode occurred in a situation highly controlled by the aliens. With each one I've encountered I've asked repeatedly about the meaning of my and others' involvement: Why me? Why us? Why, I ask myself, am I in the incredible position to be able to photograph these ships so frequently? And who am I that I can bring almost anyone with me, so that they can also observe and photograph the ships? I have received no significant understanding directly from the aliens, but I *have* arrived at some tentative—and surprising—answers that might disturb some people. My conclusions challenge many fundamental assumptions that sprang up over the last four decades since "the coming of the saucers."

The 1971 events served as preparation for what I and my colleagues were to experience in 1980. The 1980 sightings established the grounds for understanding what occurred in 1984 and into the present. This is not a subtle point; it is as if a conditioning process is occurring. The events appeared to be *planned by the aliens as if I and other contactees seem to have been chosen or targeted for it.*

This is not such a pleasant thought. On the contrary, it's frightening, disturbing. It leaves us with a sense of deepest violation, of no free will or at least a highly circumscribed one. It casts an enigmatic, even sinister, light on the subject. There's nothing wonderful about being a UFO contactee. We may be special, but there's nothing about it to inflate one's ego. So for those who think I and others are seeking publicity, glamour, fame, or fortune, from the experience, I say they couldn't be more wrong. Something happened to us that most, if not all, of us wish never did. But the situation can't be changed. It happened; the question now is where do we go from here.

With each episode, things occurred that were counter to the conventional notion of UFOs and UFO contact. I came to realize that much about UFO literature was wrong; I also saw why some of the most fundamental mistakes had been made. I was fortunate enough to see a larger picture than most writers and researchers have because their work is based on conventional assumptions, secondhand information, or perhaps a single sighting, while mine is based solely on direct observations over time.

To fully understand where my observations have led me, I must begin with a brief account of my California sightings, which concluded with the sighting of an alien inside its lighted craft. I was afraid—nearly hysterical. It so unnerved me that I felt I had to return to the comfort and security of familiar surroundings. I left the state the next day and returned to my home in New Jersey, thinking I had left the ship and its companions behind. I was wrong. The ships followed—not just me, but also many of my personal friends, to the astonishment of us all.

We humans have a fairly standardized concept of reality and life on our planet. We can accept the idea that there may be other forms of life somewhere out there. But they're not here, of course. They couldn't be. What would be your reaction if you found yourself looking point blank at what is clearly an alien spacecraft and its occupants as it flies down a quiet street while you stand on a sidewalk within an arm's length of it? For me, it ripped away all my educated preconceptions about life in the universe. The very foundation of my sense of self, personal autonomy, and free will was undermined. As I stood watching the UFO, thoughts raced through my mind that this shouldn't, *couldn't* be happening. It wasn't possible, yet there it was directly in front of me. Why? What could I have that members of an advanced alien society would want, and why were they doing it this way?

Extraordinary claims warrant extraordinary proof. So in this book I will offer what I consider to be extraordinary proof. I have taken more than 1,000 photographs of UFOs, including several showing craft on the ground with aliens around them, and I continue to take more, along with my colleagues. (Some are reproduced in the photo section and discussed in chapter 16.) Other people—just ordinary citizens—have also taken photographs and technically trained investigators, such as Dr. Harley Rutledge, chairman of the physics department at Southeastern Missouri State College, have taken quantities of photographs while performing their own study of the phenomenon. Rutledge's work, described in his *Project Identification*, and my own confirm each other's.

UFO photographs, films, and videotapes are so important because, after the inevitable hoaxes and mistakes (such as double exposures and lenticular clouds), they offer a foundation for indisputable conclusions about the reality of alien craft and their occupants. But there is a bizarre twist in the situation: *The aliens are able to control the images produced on photographs taken of their craft by surrounding the craft with shortwave radiation that obscures the craft photographically, even though it is plainly visible to the eye.* It was two years after the initial photographs were taken that I realized this was going on, and the realization was extremely unsettling. But with that insight, the UFO puzzle began to take shape. Answers fell into place.

The search for truth in this situation can only be conducted on the basis of direct experience and direct observation, not by an armchair investigation approach. It is of prime importance to get out into the night sky and look up. When people ask me, "How have you seen so many UFOs?" I reply with a question: "How many times have you been outside looking for an hour or more at the sky?" Myself and the various people I've worked with over the years in this field study of history's most important phenomenon consider ourselves fortunate to have had the opportunity, however unwillingly we were brought to it. For myself, at least, the search for understanding of the UFO phenomenon goes on. Whatever the ultimate truth turns out to be, I will accept it and attempt to communicate it. It may not turn out to be what I expected, in the manner I expected, yet I have no choice but to continue. My search still goes on.

# SILENT INVASION

# CHAPTER 1

• • •

# IN THE BEGINNING

THERE WERE LIGHTS. There were many lights—and they weren't familiar stellar bodies.

It was May, 1971. I found myself in Hollywood, California, with a friend, across the continent from my native New Jersey. We'd planned to live and work in Los Angeles. The first day in our garden apartment, residents told us UFOs were all over the sky every night and everyone sat outside watching them. My friend and I looked at each other with raised eyebrows. I had accepted the idea—intellectually, in the abstract—that UFOs were around, but this information took me by surprise.

That night we sat outside with perhaps twenty other tenants of the apartment complex, gathered around a center courtyard, looking at the sky. Several pointed to stationary objects and told us to watch them because sooner or later they would move. I kept saying, "But they look like stars." And I was told to keep watching because the "stars" would suddenly move across the sky and stop again. So I watched—and they did! There was no noise and no discernable pattern.

At any given moment, as many as thirty objects seemed to be moving in the sky. The atmosphere above the Los Angeles basin is, of course, filled with commercial and private aircraft. The moving objects I'm talking about were clearly not that sort. These objects made right-angle turns, had no noise associated with them, and seemed to be going nowhere. The activity also appeared to be centered over our area, which wasn't far from the downtown section of Hollywood. It was, in fact, only half a mile from the famed Hollywood and Vine intersection.

This activity went on night after night. Every evening as dusk began, we would sit outside watching the sky. The stars came out as they normally do, but so did lights that moved erratically around the sky and then stopped, as if they were taking their place among the stars. Everyone in the apartment complex who watched with us accepted the phenomenon as obviously extraterrestrial. They also took a strangely passive attitude toward the situation. The UFOs were there, they were fun to watch—but so what? I seemed to be the only one who wanted to know more about what we were seeing.

I also wanted to know why the media wasn't covering the situation. I couldn't believe we were the only people seeing this. Looking back, it's clear that many reports of UFOs came out of that time and place. And in the music world—I am a musician by training so I paid special attention here—many rock groups wrote songs about what they were seeing, notably the Jefferson Airplane (now Starship) and Crosby, Stills, Nash and Young. At an Emerson, Lake, and Palmer concert at the Hollywood Bowl, which I attended, UFOs flew over and everyone saw them. When the Rolling Stones gave their Altamont concert, flying saucers hovered above the crowd, and the Stones were so fascinated that they kept looking at the saucers instead of singing.

The ships began to come in closer to us. We estimated them to be below one thousand feet. They started to play what I came to call "sky games." The ships would fly in close and turn out their lights, which tended to be white or orange, and then would turn the lights back on. They also appeared to shoot out some kind of reddish plasma discharge from one craft to another. These red "shots" would continue for a while and then stop, only to restart some time later.

We also noticed that the ships responded to our conversations, even though at the time it seemed ridiculous. If there was no movement in the sky for a few minutes, someone would say, "Gee, nothing moved in a while . . ." As if on cue, a number of ships would begin to fly all at once. It looked like they were entertaining us for the night.

It wasn't until I began regular observation at closer range in Pine Bush, New York, that I realized what should have been obvious: The ships have sophisticated remote sensing equipment all over them, imperative for the security of any operation. Through audio and visual surveillance, they easily monitor what someone may say or do while viewing the ships, perhaps even using a translating device, and even going so far as to watch people's facial expressions and reactions in close encounters. *They do not read our minds telepathically;* their apparent omniscience is not due to psychic powers, although I imagine they have such, as I'll explain later. It is, as far as I can tell, attributable to technology surpassing our own by many orders of magnitude and functioning along physical principles just now becoming apparent to human science.

After a few weeks of observing the craft from our apartment complex, I decided I wanted a closer look. About a mile from our apartment was a small hill with an excellent view of the area, so my friend and I decided to go there. I told our acquaintances about it, but as soon as I talked about taking pictures of the ships, everyone started yelling that it was wrong and that no one should take photos of them. Not only were they negative about documenting this remarkable situation, they also had an attitude toward the aliens that bordered on religious worship. I was young, inexperienced and, I regret to say, easily influenced by their authoritative opinions.

At around eleven o'clock at night we climbed the hill.

After much hesitation, I had brought my 35mm camera and hoped to photograph the actual craft, not just some lights in the sky. It was only a few minutes before a set of lights descended toward us, turning off as they came closer. Soon we could clearly see the saucer shape of an unlit craft. Totally silent, it began to circle us, staying about two hundred feet or so from us. But instead of snapping off rolls of film like an experienced professional photographer, I merely took four pictures that first night, and another three the next night when we returned to the hill where the UFO behaved identically. I simply was intimidated by the people at the apartment complex who berated me for what they felt was a violation of the sanctity of the experience. They made me more nervous than the ships did and, to my regret, I lost a terrific photo opportunity.

During the two nights we were on the hill, the UFO circled us for hours. We could see other craft slightly farther away, also circling. On both nights we felt the hill shake slightly. We left in the early hours of the morning. I did not feel afraid at any time, but we didn't return to the hill again.

Some people to whom I've told this story suspect that more may have been happening on the hill than I can recall. Abduction is the most obvious possibility. I believe I was conscious the entire time, with no lapse of memory and no "missing time"—with one exception. I can't recall exactly how the ships left, whether they ascended or simply drifted away, and I blame my poor memory on the passage of time. But I am concerned with truth—not my truth but objective, empirical accounting for the facts and their meaning. So, in order to discover whether there was more to the situation than I remembered, I underwent hypnosis in 1979. The hypnotist regressed me to 1971: Certain details were freshened in my mind—things that were to become more apparent through my Pine Bush experiences—but there were no major revelations. I've never had disturbing dreams, as have some abductees, that might indicate I'd been abducted.

So, although I am a contactee with an extraordinary number of contacts, I am not, so far as I know, an abductee. Yet apparently I had a contact experience in my very early childhood, and because of that I cannot rule out abduction completely. I simply have no conscious sense of it having occurred.

What sort of contact experience? In 1980, at the beginning of my Pine Bush adventure, I met a psychic, who revealed to me a situation from my infancy of which I'd been unaware, yet which my mother was able to confirm entirely. I was in her house; we'd only just met. She closed her eyes and psychically tapped into my personal history.

"Did anything traumatic happen to you as a child?" she asked. I recalled I had been sick for about nine months, but no one knew what I had. I recalled the doctors drawing the outlines of my organs on my abdomen so my mother could point to the ones that were enlarging. I also remembered having to stay inside while my friends were outside playing, and how I watched them having fun. I told the psychic it happened when I was four.

She said I was only two. I insisted I was four. She said she could see a spacecraft beside my white house. (She'd never been to my home, but it was white at the time referred to.) She saw aliens working some dials and controls that had to do with me. I was sleeping in my crib, she added.

I said, "Well, what are they doing?"

"Healing you."

That shocked me. I said, "Just give me a date or time. I'll ask my mother what happened when I was sick, without leading her on, so I can verify this for myself." The psychic said it had occurred in April 1953.

When I got home, I asked my mother, "What happened when I was sick? How old was I? What was going on?" She told me I was about three when I started getting sick, but no one knew why. She gave me a long account of how I got sicker and sicker. At first she took me to the doctor every two weeks, then every week. By January it was twice a week. No one knew what I had except to say that my stomach was enlarged and very upset.

By March the doctor was trying to decide whether to put me into the hospital. My parents and the doctor feared I might die because I was so much sicker.

I said to my mother, "Then what?"

She replied, "One day in April you were perfectly fine." It was very strange, she said. One day I was deathly ill and overnight I was completely better. She never figured it out.

I told her what the psychic had told me. She looked at me and said, "Well, call her back and tell her she's right!"

Night after night, we sat in the courtyard and watched the ships, which appeared to be coming closer to us. I began to worry that their presence had become normal and acceptable to us. They were there every night; we had come to take them for granted. (I was to discover in Pine Bush that the locals accepted these nightly occurrences as what they appear to be—someone else's spaceships.) Their blasé attitude disturbed me: They had no urge to understand, no desire to investigate. Yet contrary to the residents' belief, nightly occurrences were *not* normal.

If what we were seeing had occurred where scientists and people could study it, this phenomenon would have made worldwide headlines, and a solution to this enigma would be much closer, I'm sure. (I'll say in anticipation of later chapters that I have strong reasons to suspect a solution is *already* known by certain elements of our government-military-scientific establishment.) As it was, I had to pursue my investigation on a part-time basis, with no outside funding and only my very modest income as a word processor and typist for a temporary employment agency to underwrite my travel expenses, photographic equipment, supplies and developing, and sundries that come up in the course of an extended research project. Although I wish it had been otherwise, I am not complaining. I did what I had to do, and I have few regrets. I wrote this book only to encourage others to come forward and provide the resources that are still needed to proceed on a larger scale with more technical equipment and personnel. It is a worthy project: a clearer understanding of human destiny and our place in the universe beckons.

Several events scared the wits out of me, and the final one sent me hurrying back to my home in New Jersey. In fact, that event is the only one I fully comprehend. Some of my other experiences in California are still not completely understandable to me, and I consider them what I call "fringe experiences." But they all seemed to be associated with the presence of UFOs and their alien occupants.

Only in recent years have I found that others have had similar fringe experiences that make no sense in conventional terms. In fact, some of the things that happened to me *still* frighten me because of their incredible implications, if they are what they appear to be. The fact that I am not alone in having experienced terrifying things offers small consolation.

For example, one day when half a dozen friends were in our living room, the door was jolted open with such force that we all jumped in fright. We immediately glanced into the corridor that ended just beyond our apartment. No one could have run away unseen, yet no one was there. Significantly, I felt a very strong "presence" enter the room. It seemed as if someone else was there. None of us moved for a few moments; we were frozen with anxiety. Our hearts were pounding because we were holding our breath in order not to make any sound. We were listening and waiting for something more. But it never happened.

On another occasion, I was sitting in the courtyard with two friends when we heard a strange sound begin at one end of the area. It was a very loud, mechanical sound with a metallic edge to it, originating in midair. The closest I can come to identifying it is this: It sounded like the chirp-click of a child's cricket toy. The sound started to travel toward us, coming *around* the perimeter of the swimming pool. It was obviously controlled and not random, not natural. We gripped our chairs in terror. The sound passed over each of us, stopped, reversed direction, then returned to its point of origin and vanished. We sat frozen in silence for a minute, then started talking all at once. My two companions said they had felt a falling sensation; so had I. I didn't hear the sound again, but several days later, the mother of the young men who heard it with me that evening heard it another night—in her apartment. And on a separate occasion in 1978, so did Sandy, one of my two sisters. I don't know what this metallic chirp-cricket sound means, but one guess is that it's some type of controlled body scan performed on humans by the aliens—another high tech aspect of the UFO experience, although it does sound like science fiction.

The final "straw that broke the camel's back" sent me flying home—in an airplane.

I worked at a part-time job within walking distance of our apartment. I would leave work at nine o'clock in the evening and walk several blocks down a residential side street to go home. One August evening about four months after I arrived in Hollywood, something made me turn around and look up. As I did, my heart skipped several beats. Above the rooftop of a small house, an angular craft was descending toward me silently. It was extremely large and a headlight shone down at me. As it glided slowly toward me, at perhaps three or four miles per hour, I froze in terror and awe.

The interior of the craft was completely lit up and I could see everything clearly, including the being sitting in the front seat. It had its hand on what looked like a joystick apparently used to control the craft. It wore what looked like a rustbrown metallic stretch-knit jumpsuit with a hood. The jumpsuit covered the back and sides of its head, as well as its body from the neck and arms down. The garment had a glittery look, and when I noticed that detail, I laughed to myself, thinking, "Oh, my God! They have stretch-knit fabric!"

Its head looked enlarged, bulbous. Its arms and shoulders were broad and very thin like a fashion model's. I don't remember specific details about the face, and that puzzles me.. I wonder whether I've subconsciously blocked the memory or there was too much to take in during the brief time I observed it, or whether I simply avoided eye contact because it would have "clinched" the experience—forcing the reality of the moment to sink in.

The front of the craft had four clear window panels, apparently glass and each larger than a car. I couldn't see the entire shape of the craft's exterior, although it was definitely angular and not the rounded saucer we had been seeing nightly. I kept looking for that familiar round shape and couldn't understand why I was seeing an angular one. It wasn't until 1980 in Pine Bush that I realized I had been looking at a triangle-shaped craft similar, but not identical, to the "boomerang" or "flying wing." The "Westchester Wing" described in J. Allen Hynek and Philip Imbrogno's *Night Siege* is perhaps the best-known UFO of this type. And I saw it in the middle of Hollywood, no less.

Multicolored flashing lights were clearly visible on what looked like computer equipment lining an inner wall of the craft. Seeing the flashing computers made the reality of the situation hit home. There were two seats in front—one (to my right) in which a being sat and another (to my left) which appeared empty, although under regressive hypnosis in 1979 I seemed to think a second being was standing next to a third being who sat in that seat. However, I'm not sure the regressive process is completely reliable, accurate, or objective unless done by a Ph.D. in psychiatry or psychology.

The craft was visible for probably no more than three minutes. No one was on the street. As I watched the craft, I realized I either had to stand still and accept any consequences or run. I ran. I could kick myself now. How could I have thought I could run from the craft?

I bolted down the street and turned to see the craft casually bobbing along next to me. To use the vernacular, I freaked out and began to cry. Without verbal communication, I had no way to know its intent, although it did seem like it was playing with me and not trying to harm me. Looking back, it must have been funny to the aliens. I was not amused.

I charged across the street to our apartment. Once inside, I proceeded to pack my clothes, sobbing hysterically. The next morning I telephoned my parents to say I was flying back that day. When I got home, though, I didn't tell my parents of my adventures. I felt inhibited around them—not an unusual situation for a twenty-one-year-old daughter—although they knew I had long been interested in the subject. I'd collected UFO articles since I was ten. However, it was not until 1980 and the beginning of my Pine Bush investigation that I broached the subject with them by showing my photographs to my mother, and then the full story came out. (They've also both seen UFOs hovering near our home, as I'll recount in chapter 7.)

I did tell my sisters and some friends, though. A week later, a girlfriend told me that she and her sister had been with their mother in a nearby baseball field around dusk when a lit object appeared in the sky above them and remained stationary for several minutes. She said it was much too low for an airplane, which couldn't have remained stationary anyway. The object then moved off. Her mother also informed me of what they saw.

Thus began a series of sightings in northern New Jersey that was to continue for about two years. At one point, upward of two dozen lights were in the sky at once, just circling around and around, never going any place. My parents' home is below a flight path to a local airport. On some nights air traffic is continuous. But planes obviously were vehicles that came and went, making noise where it was expected, winging through the sky on their way to and from the airport. The other lighted objects never seemed to be going anywhere. One could argue that they were privately owned planes with pilots flying around just for enjoyment. But we saw many lighted objects going around in circles over the area for four hours or more.

On some nights, to our amazement, some of the craft would descend to the treetops and light up so we could see what we were looking at. Sometimes I would set up my camera on a tripod in an upstairs room that overlooks the entire area and take picture after picture—with surprising and revealing results. The photographs were registering more going on in the sky than our eyes could see.

My parents have a second home in the Pocono Mountains of Pennsylvania, and on weekends the family sometimes goes there for rest and relaxation. One Sunday in October, 1971, my father and I were driving back to New Jersey with my sister's girlfriend, Jamie. Around ten o'clock at night, going south on the New York State Thruway, I noticed a peculiar light in the sky on the other side of the highway. It seemed to be moving with us.

At first my father thought it was some sort of tower light, but when we turned off the thruway onto the Garden State Parkway, we could see the light move lower and closer. As we drove onto the exit and slowed to negotiate the curved ramp, I realized it was the biggest UFO I had ever seen. It was hovering perhaps a few feet off the ground, barely out of our path. It had two huge, round, red pulsating lights. Each of them was at least as big as our car. The craft was enormous and looked as if it were surrounded by some sort of fog. We couldn't see it completely.

Jamie had dozed off. I screamed, "Jamie! Jamie!" She woke and began yelling, "I see it! I see it!"

My father slowed the car but was too confused to stop immediately. He didn't understand what he had been looking at. He has poor night vision and doesn't like to drive in the dark. When the commotion broke out, he naturally concentrated on driving safely in a situation where he had impaired vision. Jamie knew exactly what we were seeing, although the event lasted only a few seconds. My father wouldn't stop to let me out, and instead drove past the craft, leaving me very angry at the missed opportunity.

I didn't see anything more for many months. Throughout that time, however, I had the feeling that I was being watched. Call it intuition, ESP or whatever, it was the same sensation as being in a room where someone behind you stares at you and you feel it enough to turn around and find the feeling is accurate. They were watching me, I thought.

By 1974, however, I had begun to feel frustrated and even slightly disgusted with the phenomenon. My family, friends, and I were seeing the craft frequently and, on occasion, close enough to get a clear look at the ships. But that was it. It seemed like a silly but potentially dangerous game. It was too staggering to think they were only playing with us. I decided I'd had enough. I went back to college to study music and geology. I also took up astronomy and worked briefly in a planetarium. I tried to bury my UFO experiences.

When the movie *Close Encounters of the Third Kind* was released in 1977, I realized what a mistake I'd made in trying to ignore the situation. I was always aware that the implications of what I had seen were far too serious and important to ignore. I decided that if the ships flew around the California sky as they did, and then haunted me in New Jersey, there might be more areas where they were concentrated and where, as in California, I would see them at close range again. I allowed my interest free reign again and began to seek out UFO groups that might know of sightings in the area.

After reading a UFO column in *Omni*, I called the magazine to speak with the column's editor, Harry Lebelson. I briefly told him of my California experiences and mentioned that I had taken some photos. I suggested there must be other places where UFOs were being seen frequently.

Harry did know of such a place, so we agreed to meet and talk. He told me about a young couple living near Middletown, New York, who claimed to see ships all the time. (In fact, so many people had seen UFOs in the area from Middletown eastward across the Hudson to western Connecticut that one national publication called it a "UFO corridor.") Harry, who was also a field investigator for the now-defunct Aerial Phenomena Research Organization (APRO), said he had been there with a group of people, but no one saw anything. When he told me what the couple claimed was happening to them, it seemed I was hearing a repeat of my California experiences. I urged Harry to get in touch with those people to arrange an interview.

He did. Thus began my most intensive, revealing—and continuing—field study of UFOs through direct observation. And when I say "field," I mean precisely that. I was to find myself in various fields and farm pastures in pursuit of elusive, wily, but seemingly playful UFOs—and in search of answers to some very serious questions.

# CHAPTER 2

• • •

# TOUCHDOWN IN PINE BUSH

SEVERAL DAYS LATER, Harry and I drove to Pine Bush, a rural Orange County, New York, community nestled among gentle hills and valleys some sixty miles upstate from Manhattan and a drive of one and a half hours from my home. Located at the intersection of Route 302 and Route 52, Pine Bush has a 1930-ish look and is typical of the many small towns of the area, such as its neighbors of Wallkill, Walden, and Montgomery. It has a few gas stations and restaurants, variety stores, a florist, art gallery, supermarket, and so forth. From the few main paved roads, unpaved roads lead into the countryside past scenic farms and fields.

Pine Bush is actually the small downtown business section of Crawford Township. It is, technically speaking, distinct from the town of Crawford, being an unincorporated hamlet within it. To everyone but natives, this is a distinction without a difference. The town hall of Crawford has a Pine Bush mailing address, for example. So for all intents and purposes, Pine Bush and Crawford are one and the same. Crawford comprises some seven sparsely populated square miles in which about six thousand people live. An agricultural center, it consists mostly of cornfields, dairy and horse farms that produce vegetables, fruit, trotters and pacers.

Local media have reported UFO sightings in both Crawford and Pine Bush. A policeman, a barber, store clerks, and laborers—all average working-class individuals—have, as Harry put in his September 1981 *Omni* article, interacted with one aspect or another of the UFO phenomenon at least since 1969. My sightings have mainly been in the countryside of Pine Bush (with some in Wallkill and Montgomery), but people who own stores or work in downtown Pine Bush have seen UFOs directly above their businesses and offices there.

It was Friday, July 18, 1980. Arriving in Pine Bush about eight o'clock in the evening, we drove down the main street, Hill Avenue, to the home of the couple Harry knew. The house, a two-story fieldstone with a large field next to it, is secluded, although only a mile or so from the center of town. We'd hardly done more than say hello to Bruce and Wendy when they told us in plain terms they didn't want any publicity. In fact, they said they didn't want anything to do with UFOs, but would take us to the fields where the ships were landing—reluctantly and only as a favor to Harry. That was it.

"Landing?" I exclaimed. I said I had never seen ships land in California. They gave me a puzzled look. I told them I had seen ships up close in California and started to give them some details of what I experienced. Their standoffish attitude changed immediately.

They told us how afraid they were. First of all, they said, the ships had passed over their house several times, shaking it. They felt terrorized. In addition, the people Harry had previously accompanied to the house had continued their visits, abusing the couple by barging in on weekends and practically taking over. When the dozen or so people went driving down back roads looking for ships, the ships flew off in other directions. Harry interjected, by way of apology, that several of the crowd were known to be "kooky."

"Well," I said with mock seriousness, "at least the ships are showing themselves to people who have some class."

About ten o'clock P.M., Harry and I got into my car with

Bruce and Wendy, who directed us to drive east on Hill Avenue. The night was black but clear, with a thin crescent moon. A number of houses lined the road, although they were spread out with large parcels of farmland between. They are definitely not off the beaten path. Within a mile, Bruce and Wendy told me to pull over next to a field with a slight rise toward the far side. I did.

We got out of the car and looked up. Almost immediately we were surrounded by about a dozen large triangular craft with amber-yellow lights in the form of a "plus sign" on their front. The plus-sign-shaped lighting panels divided four window panels that made up most of the front of the ships. I came to call those particular lights "starlights" because, as I was soon to learn, they could be turned up to a blinding degree of illumination and could also act as a headlight or spotlight. In fact, they could be used as a pair of headlights. When the intensity of the lights was raised to full bore, the entire sky lit up.

The ships also had multicolored blinking lights all over them. I was staring at the triangular craft I had seen in California! But now, all the exterior sections I couldn't see in California were clearly visible.

I was ecstatic. My searching seemed over. I was reunited with "my" ships after nine years. I hoped I could uncover the great secrets they held. I couldn't have been happier.

The ships were filling the sky around us and landing in the field. It seemed like Grand Central Station at rush hour. Some flew as close as fifty feet, but none of them were close enough for us to see the occupants. They made no sound. The sky was too dark to make out other details.

My camera at the time was a Zenite—a Russian 35mm SLR, like a manual Pentax, with an f/2.0 lens. I'd loaded it with a thirty-six-shot roll of Kodacolor ASA 400. It was hanging around my neck, so I brought it up to shoot picture after picture. Harry had a Leica worth twelve hundred dollars, also loaded like mine, and he did the same. When I realized the ships were on the ground, perhaps two hundred feet from us, I wanted to walk to them. The four of us started walking into the field, but when we reached the end of the road's shoulder, we had to stop. The field was fallow with weeds five feet high. None of us knew the terrain. It seemed impossible to go farther.

Wendy said that if we drove, the ships would follow. Harry and I looked at each other, momentarily doubting her, but then we piled into the car and started to drive. Sure enough, as I drove along Hill Avenue, the ships began to move at treetop level, parallel to us. We were astonished. They were keeping pace with us. There was no mistake about the shape of the ships; they were clearly triangular. And completely silent.

We drove down several roads, then Wendy suggested that we drive back to their house where we could see the craft well. I wanted more than to see them well; I wanted to get directly to them. I was angry that I'd been stopped from walking up to the ships by some weeds, of all things.

I drove back on Hill Avenue and turned left onto Bruce and Wendy's dirt road. Just then a ship, fully lit in blazing amber, rose from a nearby field and came directly toward us on my side. Wendy started screaming. Harry yelled to stop the car; Bruce yelled to keep on driving.

I almost stood on the brake to stop the car. The craft came right at us. I prayed it wouldn't hit us. The last thing I needed was to tell my car insurance company I'd had an accident with a UFO. "A spacecraft hit my car," I would say. And they would say, "Yeah, lady, sure it did. . . ."

At the last moment, the ship climbed slightly and skimmed over my car. Bruce and I turned around, amid Wendy's screaming, and watched the craft through the rear window as it passed over the car. It missed us by inches. The surface of the craft looked metallic. Parts were black as onyx while other parts of it were silvery colored, the way UFOs are popularly conceived. I could also see seams in its surface, apparently where metal plates joined, as well as the rivets that held them in place. The four window panels were clearly visible, but the craft was not lit internally as it had been in California. Black metal covered portions of the craft around the front windows. That surprised me, and I later wondered if it served to reduce glare, just as our own cars have nonglare window molding.

Something was flying spaceships around our planet. Whatever the intelligence controlling the craft, I thought, they were probably thousands of years ahead of us and perhaps saw no need to announce their presence. Perhaps they even felt their presence was none of our business. They had come in silence. Whatever their mission, I said to myself, it must be incredibly important. There are too many ships for anything other than a large scale operation. I became all the more determined to find out what on earth was going on—and even, if possible, what was going on beyond earth.

It was about three o'clock in the morning when we returned to Bruce and Wendy's house. They said they were going to sleep. Harry and I stood in the back yard watching the ships flying around the treetops. I told Harry that we had to document what was going on, and that we needed help. I asked if *Omni* would help us. He laughed. His answer shocked me. *Omni*'s management, he said, doesn't believe in UFOs. They publish material about them for commercial reasons, just like any other magazine. It's strictly a business decision, having little to do with journalism and scientific research.

The next morning, Harry and I returned to the field to look for markings on the ground where ships had landed. Bruce and Wendy wanted nothing to do with the entire scene. As Harry and I stood beside our car, we noticed a dead deer lying on the grass across the street. It had apparently been hit by a car and dragged to the side of the road. We started to talk about animal mutilations in connection with UFOs. Just then a police car appeared. The officer stopped and looked us over. He said someone had called about a dead deer. We pointed to it, assuring him we'd had nothing to do with it. Then Harry asked the officer if he had seen any strange lights in the area the night before.

He looked at us with a blank expression for a moment and said, "You mean UFOs? Why, I saw them myself some years back." I gasped in surprise. He went on, "Half the police department has seen them, and the other half thinks those who've seen them are crazy." We talked briefly with him, exchanged telephone numbers, and then he left.

The policeman's name was Robert Comeau. He is no longer a member of the Crawford Police Department. On January 4, 1971, Bob was awakened by a whirring, turbine-like sound. He glanced out the window and saw a UFO hovering several hundred feet from his house. It was disc-shaped, silvery and about one hundred feet in diameter with a row of windows around a domed top—a classic flying saucer. It was visible for forty minutes, pulsating dull green to red, hovering adjacent to his house. "It made the hair on my neck stand up. It wasn't swamp gas," he told a reporter for the *Middletown Record* in 1985. Acting dutifully, he reported the sighting to his senior officer. When word got around, some on the force believed him, some didn't. At that time, Comeau was a four-year veteran officer.

I learned this information several weeks later, when Harry and I met Bob and his daughter, Yvonne, at his home. They were to appear later in the *PM Magazine* segment about the Pine Bush activities, which I describe in chapter 6. We'd arranged to speak with Bob to get more details about the craft he saw. Instead, he told us the preceding story and a lot more. Yvonne, for example, had a close encounter with a craft while driving in a truck with her boyfriend and her dog.

At the end of our interview—we taped it and all our other interviews—Bob sent us to speak with Harold

"Butch" Hunt, a barber and musician who lives in Pine Bush. Butch described several dramatic accounts that he and his friends had experienced, going as far back as the mid-1960s. We were surprised to learn UFOs had been in the area for more than fifteen years. We were even more surprised to learn later, through other interviews, that newspaper accounts of UFO sightings in the area go back more than thirty years!

One incident occurred in July, 1968, while Butch and two of his friends were crossing Red Mills Bridge in Crawford one evening. A metallic object about seventy to one hundred feet in diameter, with a row of lights around its perimeter, suddenly hovered over their car, engulfing it in light from three beams at the base of the craft. Butch told Harry and me, "I stepped on the gas and got the hell out of there as fast as I could." The men raced across the bridge with the object close behind. It followed them for a while and then was lost to sight.

In another incident several weeks later, Butch saw something else very strange in the sky while he was driving in plain daylight. He pulled his car to the side of the road and got out. A huge cigar-shaped object was floating slowly through the sky, making no sound. Even though it was about half a mile from Butch, he could clearly see a row of round windows along its middle. The object turned away from Butch and flew out of sight.

We walked into the field. The weeds that had prevented us from walking the night before turned out to be, to our dismay, a small patch on one side of a large field that had a hill but was mostly flat. We hadn't been able to see far in the dark and—talk about Murphy's law—we'd stopped beside the only part of the field where the weeds were thick enough to prevent us from entering.

As Harry and I walked through the field, we came across a perfectly circular, burned area about two feet in diameter. We simply noted it; I'm still not sure what it was. We walked toward the crest of the hill and, about thirty minutes later, found three oval, identical impressions in the ground. Each was about 2.5 feet by 3.5 feet. It was as if a giant egg had been pushed several inches into the ground. The marks measured about sixty feet apart and formed an equilateral triangle. They weren't deer beds or anything natural, as far as we could see. They were deep marks apparently made by something heavy, such as landing gear. We also saw a number of other impressions several feet in size that were gouged out and squared off. I decided they were UFO landing gear marks. I wondered about radioactivity (without worrying about exposure), and made a mental note that we needed a geiger counter and competent operator.

We photographed the marks—I refer to them as pod marks—but not the burnt circle. We were running out of film, and I figured it looked permanent enough to save it for another day—a bad assumption because several days later I couldn't find it or the pod marks, even though Harry and I combed the hill. I suspect the ships removed all traces of their presence.

We left the field for the day but returned that evening. We asked Bruce and Wendy to come along, which they did, but they refused to stay out with us for more than an hour or so, saying it was wrong to chase and photograph the ships. I'd heard that "tune" in California and felt it was foolish, so this time I was not intimidated and continued with my investigation. We saw ships flying at a distance, but encountered nothing as spectacular as the previous night's sighting. We saw them change the intensity of their lights, as if they were using a rheostat. We also saw some beams shining downward, like searchlights.

Over the weeks, Harry and I felt we ought to check with local airports, so he made some calls to them. We also bought topographical maps of the area. We learned there were only two sizable airports nearby. Orange County Airport, in Montgomery, is about four miles south of the Hill Avenue fields. It is an uncontrolled airport that is basically closed every night from nine o'clock, after the nighttime rush hour air traffic, until seven o'clock the next morning. Air traffic has increased to eighty-five thousand aircraft movements per year from about eighty thousand in 1980— enough for pilots to be concerned about it and for the airport director to talk about a control tower. Up to one hundred thousand takeoffs, landings, and practice runs occur yearly there. Although it sounds like a lot of traffic, it's accounted for by a small number of planes doing a lot of flying.

Stewart International Airport in New Windsor is about fifteen miles east-southeast of the fields. It used to contain Stewart Air Force Base. Military pilots would occasionally fly west from it to Wallkill and drop parachute trainees onto a large area used only for such drops and military exercises. But the base was closed in 1981 and now has nothing more than a few barracks. Although the airport at Stewart is international, it is very quiet with almost no air traffic at night even though more flights are now being flown in and out than previously. Air traffic controllers there have told us that most of the air traffic we saw in the area was heading toward Newark Airport in New Jersey.

One air controller, Tom Vicarro, told Harry during a fact-finding conversation that he was on duty one night in 1980 when he received a call from the airport's operations supervisor. Someone at the *Record* had said the paper was getting calls from people about a UFO sighting and wanted to know whether the tower had spotted anything. Viccaro looked out the window nearest him, scanned the sky, but didn't see anything unusual, and said so. About thirty minutes later operations notified him that someone had just called to report a UFO over the same area. Viccaro told Harry, "When I was notified of this, I decided to go over to the other side of the tower to take another look. What I saw was a very bright light hovering in the sky. It was much too intense and enormous in size to have been a star or a planet."

Viccaro also said that pilots and airport personnel saw the ships frequently and that the Pine Bush area was not covered at all by radar. It was a border area, and the closest radar stations were at Cleveland and Long Island airports. I wondered whether the lack of radar was a key to identifying what appear to be rendezvous areas. The Pine Bush rendezvous area seemed to have about fifty ships of various sizes and shapes "stationed" there. When Harry called the Middletown *Times-Herald Record* to ask some questions, we were astonished to learn it had many stories and accounts of UFO sightings dating back to the early 1960s.

Over the next month we returned to Pine Bush several times a week, and always the ships "greeted" us in their ambiguous but seemingly playful fashion. One especially memorable incident occurred on July 26. Harry and I had driven out Hill Avenue toward the border of the next town, just to look around. Bruce and Wendy came along in their truck, accompanied by three friends on two motorcycles. It was twilight. The sky was electric blue. Everyone had pulled over, and we stood beside my car, talking. All of a sudden, a huge triangular craft came into sight, moving slowly and noiselessly across the sky overhead. We held our breath, transfixed by the spectacular sight. The craft could be seen clearly in detail, right down to the seams in the metal. It was unlit except for two tiny round ball-shaped lights at the center of its underside—a small red light and a slightly larger green light. It had a diffused glow around it, different from lighted panels.

We could see the bulky curvature of its sides. It seemed to be about sixty feet in length, just as the pod marks we'd seen indicated. Our mouths hung open as we watched this silent beauty move across the sky at about fifteen miles per hour. What a sight! It took at least a full minute to pass over our heads. We were so frozen, staring at the sky, that our cameras hung uselessly around our necks. None of us got any photos.

Over the following weeks I drove the sixty-five miles to

Pine Bush three nights a week. Harry always accompanied me. As I drove around the area, we saw ships coming out of various fields. Whenever we spotted some activity, I parked the car and we got out to walk through the field. I started to drive around to locate other sites, and soon found a number of spots where ships seemed to appear frequently.

The first night I went looking for other landing sites, we found a field northeast of Pine Bush on Route 52 with a flat-topped hill that looked like it would give us a good view of the terrain. A large number of fields stretched beyond the field we were in.

We stood on the crest, taking in the view. We could see lights around the treelines, but nothing was visible at close range. An aircraft came into view at the far side of the field. It looked like a small private plane. In California, my friends and I had watched an airplane fly into the vicinity of a group of UFOs. To our astonishment, as the plane approached a ship that seemed to be in the plane's path, the ship shot straight up. The plane passed, and the ship descended to its previous position. The same thing now happened. The plane came toward a craft and must have seen some type of light ahead, not knowing what it was. It bore down directly on it. The ship turned off all its lights, dropping quickly in altitude. Harry and I were amazed; I imagine the pilot must have been even more so. The plane jerked in its flight path, wavering as it ascended, then turned and continued on its way. The UFO remained in the same location, turning its lights on again.

I had parked my car just off the road on a dirt shoulder. As we stood surveying the scene, we saw a police car stop at the car. I sighed, not wanting interference at such a critical moment. Just then we heard something behind us on the far side of the field. We turned to see a ship lifting off from the field we were in—maybe 150 feet from us. It had some small lights on and didn't make a sound.

I shouted, "Harry, don't move. I'll take care of the cops." I ran down the hill, but Harry was right behind me.

He said, "I'm not staying up there alone!"

It was a local policeman. He'd stopped to see if we were stuck or in some kind of trouble. We stood at the far edge of the highway shoulder, with the officer facing us, looking away from the hill. We said everything was all right. Then Harry asked him if he'd seen any UFOs in the area. And at that very moment, coming down the hill in back of him were the lights of the craft we'd seen in the field. He laughed and said he hadn't. Then he got into his cruiser and drove away. The craft, approaching slowly, came to the road where we were and stopped. It changed its lighting system again to other types of lights—all large and at places all over the craft. In fact, the entire ship seemed to have all colors of lights in various combinations on every part of it. The aliens could change the lights in any manner, and we could see why people could mistake their shapes if the lights defined only portions of the vehicle. Even more important, the aliens could imitate aircraft lights. (I've pointed out these lights to people, explaining that they were UFOs, only to be told they were just airplanes. Now, I'm not saying that every airplanelike set of lights in the night sky is a UFO, but I am saying the aliens can mimic them to deceive us and have done a great job of airplane imitations. Why they do, I don't know, but it is part of their game.)

The craft started to veer around us and move across another field. We got in the car and followed it back to the first field. It came sailing by us slowly and suddenly turned head-on to us, flashing the large yellow-amber plus-sign-shaped front lighting panel off-on, off-on, off-on. Then it silently turned away from us and headed down a treeline. Harry started yelling to it to come back. He said to me, "See, they *do* flash their lights to communicate with us."

I reflected for a moment and then, suddenly, a thought struck me like lightning. As we had driven past the other fields that evening, we talked about Betty Hill's continuing contact with aliens. (Betty's story is told in John Fuller's bestseller, *The Interrupted Journey.* In 1961 she and her husband, Barney, were abducted on a deserted New Hampshire road. The story was dramatized in a 1978 movie for television, *The UFO Incident.*) What isn't widely known is that Betty has continued to see craft in the vicinity of her Portsmouth home. On occasion she has flashed her car lights at the ships because she wasn't having any other, more direct conversations with the aliens. Only this communication method had worked for her; the aliens had flashed back. Harry learned this by phoning her for advice on what we should do. But I refused to take her advice and flash our car lights. If the aliens wanted to talk with me, they could do it verbally, not through flashing lights. They may have been in control of the situation, but they were not in control of my will or my values—and I wanted direct, comprehensible contact.

Harry and I had been discussing Betty's advice, and the aliens had heard that conversation! It dawned on me that they had heard *all* our conversations, as well as other people's. There was nothing psychic about it, as Harry and others believed. The aliens had to have audiovisual surveillance equipment for their own security. If someone unknowingly walked toward a ship in a field, the ship had to know who was coming and what the intent was. Therefore, they must use optical as well as audio devices. And I imagine they have other forms of surveillance technology that operate along different lines.

They knew I wanted one-to-one contact and wanted it badly. I wanted to go aboard a ship for a ride. I wanted to learn their secrets, to understand the cosmos from their level of knowledge. When I realized most fields were accessible, I was determined to walk into any field that might have a ship sitting in it. The aliens had to have their guard up. I didn't know if these seemingly playful beings were dangerous, but simple prudence required me to be careful. Radiation was a possibility; I had also heard stories that ships have occasionally crashed. With those thoughts in mind, I wasn't going to jeopardize my life or anyone else's.

So the ship had flashed its large front light at us in an apparently deliberate move to enlighten me to the fact that the occupants had heard our conversation. Why? Did they want to do more but were not "allowed" to contact us directly?

When I started to think about how, at times, we had yelled and cursed at the ships for not doing what we wanted and how we told dirty jokes while standing in the fields to pass the time, I began to feel self-conscious about what the aliens were really thinking of us. I didn't want to communicate with them this way. I didn't want *anyone* eavesdropping on me, and least of all them. But the entire notion of meeting aliens and dealing with them in the classic manner of "take me to your leader" had to be discarded; they were already here and not at all in the manner we thought they should be. We humans, myself included, had thought that encountering extraterrestrial life would be a momentous occasion. The ETs, it seems, thought otherwise. They had their business to perform and were simply doing it; judging only from my own experience, humans seemed rather superfluous to the situation.

I emphasize my own experience because the experience of hundreds of UFO abductees, as chronicled by Budd Hopkins in his very important book, *Intruders*, certainly indicates otherwise. In his view, humans are crucial to the survival of an alien race that is conducting genetic experiments on us. All I can say is that my many contacts with UFOs provided plenty of opportunities for abduction, but I was never abducted. They only toyed with me. Perhaps they involved me for a totally different purpose, even though I *wanted* to be abducted—i.e., taken aboard for a meeting. I believe the aliens are here for reasons that, if ever truly known, will be staggering to human thought. In view of all the cattle mutilations allegedly caused by them, they could indeed be performing biological experiments, just as Hopkins concludes. What the aliens are ultimately here for remains to be seen.

By mid-August we had been to Pine Bush three to four nights a week for a month. Because of a drought in the area, every night was clear and dry. We had seen hundreds of triangular ships or at least, since we hadn't gotten their license plate numbers, had seen numbers of triangular ships dozens of times. Upward of thirty ships seemed to be in the sky at once each night. Some of our outstanding sightings occurred at dusk when the sky was still light. And some of those had been observed by some friends of Bruce and Wendy who came out to the fields with us.

Meanwhile, I'd sent my initial roll of film to a local Fotomat store. When I got the pictures back, Harry and I stared at the bizarre bursts of multicolored lights they showed. Sprays of shooting discharges and splashes of different hues were all over the frames. The first three pictures on the roll were of my home and family, so there was no question that the film was mine and that it was normally processed. But where were the triangular ships with the yellow plus-lights we had so clearly seen? I had gotten fourteen images of the ships; the others were blank. Harry's were completely blank. And it was to be the case that he *always* got blanks, although we couldn't understand why since he is a competent photographer. (I have some ideas about that which I'll present in chapter 15.) A couple of my photos did have lights from some of the ships, but they still weren't what we actually saw.

To help us understand the situation, Harry wrote a letter to the "Reader's Forum" section of *Photomethods*, which published it in October 1982, along with two of my photos. He briefly described our experience, stating, "The photographs were taken for evaluation to Columbia University, Rockefeller University, Rutgers University, Stevens Institute of Technology, and Montclair State College. Only a few scientists offered comments based on their scientific expertise and not on their personal opinions about the subject.''

Their comments were more helpful in telling me what the phenomenon wasn't than what it was. Astronomer Robert Jastrow at Columbia University said, ''I'm unable to interpret these images as atmospheric electricity. They may be something totally unknown to us at this time.'' Harry included Jastrow's comment and ended the article by inviting scientists interested in examining the photos to contact us. None did.

Two years elapsed before I figured out what was going on in my photos. During that time I read all the physics textbooks I could find. I also talked with many scientists in nearby universities and businesses. When I finally established what my photographs showed, I also realized that the information I had probably pertained to every UFO photo during the past forty-plus years, when the modern era of the phenomenon began. And what I discovered wasn't psychic mumbo-jumbo; it was physical—some of it straight out of physics books. Moreover, I realized that if I—a composer, finishing a Ph.D. in music composition at New York University who minored in science on the undergraduate level—could figure out the situation, then the many experts involved in military and government studies of the phenomenon should certainly have known long ago what was occurring.

I will describe the situation fully in chapter 15. I mention it here because when I got my photos back from the store, Harry used them as proof that a psychic phenomenon was occurring. Harry had two twelve-hundred dollar Leicas that worked perfectly in frequent tests photographing daytime landscapes, yet he got blanks. From my perspective, nothing psychic was going on. The ships were mechanical, albeit with sophisticated technology, and the aliens were living, biological entities. Everything that occurred between them and us took place in the same familiar three-dimensional space I used along with everyone else to drive my car, talk with my friends and parents, eat food, play music, wash clothes, and so forth. Harry and others wanted to mystify the whole thing and never tired of trying to convince me of a psychic dimension surrounding our experiences. I won't deny that there may be a psychic dimension to it. After all, hundreds of contactees tell of telepathic communications with aliens, dematerializations in which they are abducted and taken through solid walls into spaceships. But on the basis of my own experience, I assert that most, if not all, of what occurs is not supernatural—it's simply supertechnological. Just because we don't understand the mechanics of what's happening doesn't mean it is psychic.

In fact, I became so suspicious of the facile psychic explanation that I went through great effort to analyze every aspect of every close encounter I had. I wanted answers for myself—answers that had the ring of truth, not fuzzy-minded escapism or glib New Age nonsense. One way or another, I was going to get those answers. My research indicated a point where it appears we are watching aliens that are able to control electromagnetic fields that are physical and measurable. Quite obviously, they use them in conjunction with their ships. They may also use them to influence us. They may be able to tap into our biological energy fields—an aspect of the human aura—for communication purposes, to immobilize us, to block pain, and to create the other effects that contactees and abductees have reported. We are electrical systems, and the aliens apparently have advanced technology to "plug in" to us and do things of which we have little or no understanding. I've already mentioned the situation in which you suddenly get the feeling that someone is watching you. How a person can feel that is not clearly understood, but I suspect it has to do with the person's brainwaves and body fields intermingling with another's. (Research on auras is being done through kirlian photography.) Aliens appear to have achieved a remarkable understanding of human physiology and psychology, and they have sufficient technological control to do pretty much as they please with us.

In this light, it is easy to regard the aliens in their ships as a godlike presence. Yet that would be naive. They may represent a technology one thousand or more years ahead of us, but gods from outer space they are not, even though they evoke religious feelings in some people. The impression of divinity is deepened by their cryptic behavior. They seem deliberately to give notice of their presence, sometimes obliquely, sometimes overtly, even to the point of blatantly leaving evidence such as landing marks, radiated soil, broken tree branches, etc. But they are selective in who sees them and what is seen. In my case, I was being given direct, repeated contact. Why? They were disrupting my life, and if these interactions had a purpose, I wanted to know what it was. I was determined to find out.

# CHAPTER 3
• • •
# A PHYSICIST OFFERS HELP

IN THE FIRST week of August, Harry invited a friend, a graduate student in physics, to accompany us. Samuel Stecher attended Stevens Institute of Technology in Hoboken, New Jersey. (He has since moved to Arizona, where he works as a physicist and inventor.) Sam and I had met several weeks earlier through Harry. I liked him, thought he could help the research, and was glad to have him along. I mentioned the pod marks, so he borrowed a fifteen-hundred dollar geiger counter from his department to bring along, as well as a Nikon camera and a 400mm lens. Clearly I needed as much help as I could get, especially from professional scientists and technicians.

In time I was to have dozens of people accompany me—friends and relatives, people who wrote to me or called and simply showed a sincere interest in the phenomenon, people who'd had UFO sightings elsewhere, psychics who thought they could back up my ability with their own perceptions, journalists, media personalities (even a crew from TV's now-defunct *PM Magazine*). On a few occasions I've had as many as fifteen people in a field at once. On some evenings the people have seen what I've seen; I've collected statements from them, which I reproduce in Appendix 1. Nearly all those incidents took place from 1984 onward, however. In the first period of my Pine Bush research, my only companions were Harry and, occasionally, Sam, plus a few local people.

At dusk, the three of us headed for the hill where Harry and I had seen the pod marks. I refer to it as the first site. We went up the hill to what looked like a day-old pod mark. Sam put the geiger counter's sensor near it. The needle jumped off the scale. We all laughed at first, but quickly sobered up as we realized the seriousness of what that reading meant. Sam tried to take another reading but couldn't get the geiger counter to work again. (His department had to have it repaired, and he was forbidden to borrow it again.)

We drove away from the first site, heading for Route 52. A craft with a huge yellow-white light came down directly in front of us across the street and went behind some trees.

I yelled gleefully, "Our welcoming committee!"

Sam flipped out, exclaiming, "Oh, my God. . . ." It was not the last time I was to hear a newcomer gasp in amazement at the mere appearance, let alone the breathtaking beauty, of the ships.

I turned onto Route 52 and headed for our destination— the hilltop where the craft had lifted off right behind us in the field. I refer to that location as the second site. Arriving there, I decided to drive my car into the field and park behind a fence. I figured no one would see the car and I wouldn't have to worry about the police coming by. (I was proven wrong several weeks later when the owner of the field confronted us with trespassing and I had to explain my purpose in being there. He was skeptical, but gave me permission to go on his land. From then on, I made a point of getting permission from landowners whenever I went into new fields. In time, I became so familiar to local merchants and the police force that most people knew what I was doing out there at night. In fact, people often drove by to discuss recent sightings.)

We began dragging all our equipment up the hill. At the top, we turned around to survey the scene. The UFO we had just seen was lifting up from the trees where we'd seen it. We now had an excellent view.

It came toward us with a red light on. We stood still, watching. It halted in midair about 250 feet from us. As usual we couldn't see its shape. Sam was going wild with disbelief. The craft was perfectly stationary above the road.

Sam said, "What's it doing?"

I replied, "It must be checking us out."

It suddenly occurred to me that the aliens were looking us over as if they were thinking about where else they could land so that we wouldn't be in their way. I distinctly realized that they weren't going to land in the field and had to decide where to go. I felt as if I had just discovered a puzzle piece and fitted it into the right place or had figured out how a mystery story was going to end.

Sam began to walk farther into the field. I said to him, "Wait. Don't go any farther. They're not going to land here. They're going to another field."

He laughed derisively and asked, "How do *you* know?" I told him it looked obvious. But the feelings I'd had that led to that knowledge were apparently anything but obvious.

The ship turned east and proceeded down the tree line bordering the road. We were north of the ship and the trees. Then it crossed the road to our side and was joined by a group of two or three other ships. A minute later the ships had gathered together one field east of us, perhaps half a mile away. There they proceeded to put on a light show for us. Some lights were steady, others blinked in multiple colors.

I noticed that the craft had followed the contour of the tree line. I realized it must be for camouflage purposes. They would be more difficult to see and could easily duck into the trees to avoid being seen if necessary. I've never seen their behavior change. In every location where I've seen ships, they tend, for the most part, to stay over trees, following the contours of tree lines that divide fields and border roads.

I mentioned my discovery to Harry and Sam. They looked around at the tree lines. There were four—one in each direction—with an awful lot of lights curving up and down the contours of the hills. Airplanes fly in straight lines, making noise if low in the sky and, often, contrails, when higher. Their path is predictable and unremarkable. But now we could see the ships moving along the curve of the hills, hugging the trees. This pattern of behavior became our sure means of spotting UFOs at a distance and distinguishing them from conventional aircraft, which moved across the sky high above the trees on relatively straight courses. The UFOs seemed to move in circles around the area.

To verify my identification of a distant light as a UFO, I would have other people with me watch it continually to see what happened. Almost invariably, it would circle around the area for several hours, and then fly toward the other landing fields—completely out of the flight path of the planes that came through. During that time, we would not lose sight of it, so it wasn't a case of inadvertantly picking up another light in the same area. My associates and I observed UFOs in this manner too often to be mistaken.

Harry, Sam, and I watched what we thought was a plane coming toward us. It made a sound like a bee droning. It was moving very slowly—so slowly that I began to get suspicious. A short while later the "plane" came skimming over the treetops with dual headlights on. It turned so that the headlights swept across the field where we stood.

Nothing was in the field at that moment except us. The now-silent craft came toward us with those bright headlights. We stood frozen, not understanding what we should do, if anything, except watch. The craft curved slightly around us and flew in the direction of the first site. As it disappeared, we saw another craft lift off from the back of the field where the light show had been, but it didn't come near us.

The sky was beginning to get cloudy. We decided to go to the first site to see what was happening. We lugged all the equipment back to the car, drove back to Hill Avenue, and set up the equipment on the grass next to the road. As we did, a craft showing dual headlights—apparently the same one we had just seen—came skimming over the trees toward us from the direction of the second site. And when I say "skimming," I mean precisely that. Often we could see the tops of trees move as a craft brushed them.

The headlighted craft came toward us over the low hill next to us. It was perhaps fifty feet in the air, if that, sweeping its lights over the ground where we'd seen ships land. It stopped dead for about a minute, shining the beams over the ground before us. We didn't know if we were supposed to respond.

The ship then came toward us. We panicked. As the lights swept over us, Sam pushed Harry and me to the ground in an unsuccessful attempt to escape the lights. The craft was completely silent, even though it was lower than the trees, not much higher than a telephone pole. Despite its nearness, we couldn't see the shape of the craft—only the distinct round headlights and the searchlight beams moving over the ground. Soon it moved on and disappeared, leaving us to calm our shattered nerves.

Our fear abated, and in its place I felt annoyance at the "games aliens play" and the fact that our contacts never went further. Later, when we related the incident to Bruce and Wendy, they told us that they also had been caught in headlight beams on several occasions and never felt in danger. They assumed they were being checked out. It appeared from their familiarity with the situation that they were holding back a lot of information, and Harry and I were to pull some startling accounts out of them, with much difficulty. (We eventually realized their reticence was due to their quasi-religious attitude toward the ships, like my acquaintances in California. Bruce and Wendy believed our behavior toward the ships was wrong, that we shouldn't photograph them or try to study them scientifically because it wasn't appropriate for what they considered to be a spiritual situation.)

That evening Sam told me he was shooting pictures through the 400mm lens at 1/2000th of a second in order to stop the action. I told him he couldn't possibly get night shots at that speed. I had shot at 1/30th of a second. Guess what? Neither of us got anything. I couldn't understand why. The ships were bright. We were able to get airplanes on the film. There seemed no reason why we couldn't register UFOs unless—as we were to discover after months of intensive field work—they were deliberately preventing it by disturbing the emulsion of the film through means of which we were unaware.

The next night we were back in Pine Bush. Four ships gave us a show at the first site, and again one of them began to sweep the ground with its lights and come directly toward us. Again we ducked and this time managed to escape the beams. If they wanted to see us, they would have to land and get out—or invite us in. The craft turned around and flew back toward the second site, where the other ships were now gathered.

We went to the second site. The ships were following the contours of the tree lines. None came close to us. We began to notice occasional glows behind the tree line east of us. After a glow, dogs would bark. For a while, we didn't understand what we were looking at. Then we noticed a sequence of events taking place. First, a small red light would appear to come to the ground, behind trees. Then we would see a white glow, and in that area dogs barked and frogs croaked. It was eerie until I remembered that animals have extended senses far more perceptive than our own. I wondered if I could use them as a kind of radar system. As I followed this line of thought, I developed some ideas I wanted to experiment with. Progress often involves uncertainty, and I felt I had to begin taking risks.

From then on I paid attention to animal reactions. I observed animal reactions for a long time before I felt confident to say that animals and insects react in specific ways to particular situations involving UFOs.

I discovered that dogs bark when the ships land near them, though not too close. But if a ship comes by so a dog can see it, or if aliens are apparently out of their ship, dogs cower silently. When the ships take off, the dogs bark again.

Frogs make noise when the ships are close to them, whether in the air or on land. In other words, they appear unaffected.

Crickets don't make noise when the ships are on the ground, and they, more than dogs, have alerted us in fields by their silence that something is near. Crickets do not chirp when I enter a field with a ship close by, and they suddenly stop chirping when I have been in a field for some time and a ship converges on the site. It is unnerving to stand in a field noisy with insects and have them suddenly become silent when nothing can be seen.

The night was late, and we were getting bored. Sam wanted to come back with foolproof equipment for getting clear photos of the craft that bypassed the lights. He said he would talk with other professors in his department to find something or some way to do the trick. Although he could see that the Pine Bush activity involved UFOs—which were a wholly new ball game for science—he nevertheless wanted to remain within his discipline. A scientific approach to the situation was necessary, even when the UFO technology obviously surpassed our own by many orders of magnitude. I, of course, agreed, despite the feeling of relative helplessness in the face of such an advanced race of beings. As things turned out, Sam did not come up with what he'd hoped for. But that disappointment was offset by some unexpected discoveries. First, however, I was to have one of the most astounding experiences of my life.

# CHAPTER 4

. . .

# CONTACT!

ABOUT A MONTH after my first experience, I decided to go to Pine Bush alone. When I mentioned this plan to some friends, they thought I would be abducted. Going alone would be the perfect invitation for aliens to take me, they said worriedly. I had decided that the aliens could have taken me at any time, but since they hadn't, they probably weren't interested. If my fate was to be abducted the night I went alone, so be it. I felt apprehensive about personal safety, but not fearful. I wanted to experiment. It was a calculated risk, not reckless abandon. I needed to find out what was going on and what my relationship with the aliens truly was. It seemed to require going solo, so I picked a night and went.

It was more than mere scientific or intellectual curiosity that drew me. During the week or so before, I had felt a strong pull to be in Pine Bush every night. I couldn't be there because I was attending college courses and had a part-time job. But I could feel the presence of the ships tugging at me, daring me to meet with them. This awareness became stronger, yet my skepticism was also strong. I needed clarification, so I decided to calm myself and try to sort out what was going on within me.

What I perceived startled me. I suddenly felt an overwhelming wave of compassion and love from the occupants of the ships. It was an amazing revelation, and I was compelled to reciprocate. It seemed similar to suddenly discovering that another person, till then largely a stranger, loves you.

Not only was I unaware of this dimension until then, but I had been strongly focused in another direction. I had been trying to separate the psychic aspect of the UFO experience from the physical aspect and was fairly sure that what others insisted was psychic or mystic was, very simply, high tech. Their explanations didn't fit my observation. Yes, I was—and still am—psychic, but in these circumstances, I questioned the term "psychic." I was "in tune" with the aliens in the same manner that someone is attuned to a spouse, best friend, or beloved pet. The person knows how the other thinks, feels, reacts because the other is known. I had feelings about the aliens because, on some level, I had dealt with them and saw how they behaved, perhaps much as a doctor observes a patient's behavior. I was deeply surprised to learn I had strong emotional bonds with whoever was in the ships; I was equally surprised to find the feelings were mutual.

At about 9:30 P.M. on Thursday, August 7, I got off the highway and headed toward town. The only rule I imposed on myself was not to walk into a "new" field alone. Small streams, heavy brush, and livestock were too dangerous. When my friends and I had walked past barbed wire fences, we had no idea whether cattle or crops were in the field. One night we met a bull who started snorting and charging around the field, and we had to go over the fence in a hurry. It must have been a comical sight to the aliens, and I didn't want to repeat that undignified move.

I went to the field where I'd first seen UFOs. It was a moonless night, very dark and clear with stars filling the sky. I stood there nervously, looking around. Lights in the sky were moving at treetop level, but none of them were really close. I turned around to look across the street and there, quite gloriously, was a fully lit ship among the trees.

It descended into the trees and turned off all its lights.

So, there was the ship in a new field! I felt as if the aliens were baiting me to see if I would stick to my original plan of no new fields alone. I didn't take the bait, if that is what they intended. Instead, I decided to drive to the second site where I'd seen UFOs, about a mile away. I started to walk up the second hill, but withdrew and returned to my car. Whether I felt ''bad vibes'' or simple nervousness, I can't say. My mind kept wandering back to the ship at the first site, which I thought was probably still sitting there. I drove around for a while and got lost—I was to do this on many occasions in the course of familiarizing myself with the roads and terrain—but soon found my way back.

It was about one o'clock in the morning when I returned to the first site and parked at the edge of the road. What could I do with the ship I knew was sitting in the woods? I was procrastinating, partly due to fear, partly due to ignorance about the situation. As I glanced around, I noticed my flashlight and had an idea. I would roll down the passenger window and drive as slowly as I could beside the woods, shining my light into it. Then, when the beam shone on the metal craft, I would get out and knock on the door. I thought I had figured out a simple, effective plan; it didn't work out that way. I wasn't mentally prepared for what was about to occur.

I started to drive, shining the light into the trees and ground. When I came to a small clearing, my light caught something that looked like a fluttering moth. It was moving across the clearing. But as I watched it seeming to glow in the beam, I realized something was wrong with the moth.

I strained to see it clearly. Slowly, I moved the light downward from the glowing object. There was some movement beneath it—something that looked like limbs moving. ''It must be an animal,'' I thought. I continued to move my light downward and then saw a thin pair of legs. My realization that something was wrong quickly got stronger. This was no ordinary animal. Only two legs were visible.

I moved the light upward and could see a skinny neck and beige body, which gave the appearance of wearing a tightly fitting jumpsuit. Then I saw arms moving the way a person's would while running.

The "thing" ran about twenty feet across the clearing to the trees where the ship must have been and then stopped, turned and stared directly at me. It was about twenty-five feet away. I was dumbfounded. It was an alien, fully visible. I could see every detail. The "moth" my light had caught was actually the being's huge eyes that wrapped around the sides of its head to its ears. The eyes had dark pupils, like ours, but where ours are white, its were yellow and similar to a cat's eyes with their nighttime glow. Unlike a cat's eyes, however, these were diamond-shaped but more angular, like a stretched-out diamond. The being looked to be about three or four feet tall. It was slender and weighed perhaps thirty pounds.

But what utterly amazed me was the expression on the alien's face. It had a worried look as if it were thinking, "Oh, oh, I'm in trouble!" I felt totally confused. I thought, "What the hell is *it* worried about? *I* should be worried. In fact, I *am* worried!" I probably showed it, too. My chest was pounding; I felt I was falling apart at the seams.

It stood there motionless for perhaps thirty seconds, as we stared at one another. I said, "Hey . . . hey . . ." which came out as a grunt because I was choked up. It didn't answer. If it had come forward instead of staying at the field's edge, I might have left the car for a face-to-face encounter. But it didn't—and I didn't. Instead, I did one of the dumbest things I've ever done in my life: I pushed the panic button. I didn't get as hysterical as I did in California in 1971, when I'd cried at my first sight of an alien. But panic, I did. I said to myself, "Hey . . . hey . . . I'm getting out of here." I hit the accelerator and took off.

I raced to the parking lot of a nearby supermarket and looked at my watch. It was two o'clock in the morning. I sat there with the engine off, asking myself "Why, why,

why?'' It wasn't supposed to happen this way. Something was very wrong. I had simply wanted to touch a metal craft, to work into the situation slowly and carefully—not to have an alien thrust before me when I wasn't ready. What were aliens doing running around our farm fields? And most of all, why was this little creature who probably had a technology ten thousand years ahead of us—why was *it* worried about *me?*

I sat there for about an hour, calming down, unable to drive. As my mind ranged over the situation, I reviewed various pieces of UFO research I'd read. I focussed particularly on UFO researcher Leonard Stringfield, author of *Situation Red*, which contains accounts from military personnel alleging government retrieval of crashed UFOs and their alien occupants. It also has sketches of the aliens' facial features. According to what I had just seen, they were not completely accurate. The eyes shown in Stringfield's illustrations were not big enough. They didn't go far enough around the head. And the pupil wasn't circular but almost banana-shaped or like an elongated diamond.

Then my attention shifted to my friends and parents. I realized I had to tell them, especially Harry. I thought, "Oh, boy. How am I going to do this?" I had come to Pine Bush to make contact with aliens, I'd had the opportunity, but in a moment of fear, I'd thrown it away. The fact that many other people—perhaps most—might act the same way was no consolation. I'd behaved stupidly. I should have gotten out of the car and walked toward the alien. What was I so afraid of? And why was the alien itself apparently so worried? Did I surprise it? Using my flashlight was a spur-of-the-moment idea. Perhaps the alien knew I was coming down the road and had already started running back to the ship. If I had not shone the light into the woods and clearing, I would never have seen it.

I seized on the idea. Perhaps the flashlight was a spontaneous move that the alien or aliens hadn't expected. Maybe that's why the one I saw looked worried. What a thought! If true, they couldn't read our minds! *They could only predict our actions based on previous observations.*

But another aspect of the situation puzzled me. The alien could have ducked into the bushes around the field, yet it didn't. An animal knows to head for the nearest cover when it is frightened or threatened. The alien stayed in the clearing and ran across the entire field, with my flashlight on it the whole time. Was the episode staged like many other encounters appeared to be? It was puzzling—and also, in retrospect, laughable—like a scene out of a movie.

I drove home, went to bed, and although it was quite late when I went to sleep, I woke up the next morning as soon as I heard my parents up and about. I had to tell them first that I'd seen an alien. They looked at each other. My mother said gently, as only a mother can, "Are you sure?"

About midmorning, I called Harry. He thought I was joking until I told him in detail what had happened and convinced him that I would never kid about something like that. Contact with the aliens was precisely what we were looking for. We decided to go back to Pine Bush that night.

A few days later I telephoned Stringfield to discuss my experience. He said that many types of humanoids have been reported and they had different sized eyes, or at least a variety of eye shapes and sizes—a far greater variety than humans have. Though he didn't know why, he and others have speculated that the beings seen in the ships may not be the original life form of their planet(s). It may be they were "manufactured" specifically for space travel. Since UFOs come out mainly at night, the aliens' large eyes may be night-adapted, enabling them to see best then. The small size of the aliens is another feature widely noted, ideal for space travel. Since they seem to have minimal musculature, muscular atrophy during interstellar voyages would be unlikely. Their small stature would also require a relatively smaller amount of space and food. The large size of their heads implies highly developed brains, possibly with mental or psychic abilities only beginning to be seen among humanity.

The notion of engineering beings for space travel was staggering to think about. Only the aliens could provide the ultimate answers to my questions. And in order to get the answers, I would have to make contact again. I therefore vowed that I'd never let fear overcome me or run away from a close encounter again.

# CHAPTER 5

### • • •

# THE INVISIBILITY FACTOR

HARRY AND I were back in Pine Bush the evening after I saw the alien. I always had excellent intuition about which fields the ships were in, so we quickly found them. They were flying all over the sky, and I began to see some patterns developing. The ships seemed to follow the contours of the tree lines, as I'd first noticed a month earlier. For the most part, however, the evening was uneventful. We visited both the first and second sites, but nothing unusual happened—if merely seeing UFOs at a distance was routine. We left about 1:30 A.M.

The next night was one to remember. The sky was clear when we arrived about 9:15 P.M. at the first site. Ships were circling the hill at a distance. We also saw two meteors hurtle through the sky—thick, solid bands of burning debris, one white, the other orange.

About an hour later we went to the second site and saw ships everywhere—twenty or so in the sky, flashing lights of all types and moving slowly and silently along each line of trees. We began to notice more meteors. Then it occurred to me that it was the time of year for the Perseid meteor shower, which produces upward of fifty meteors per hour for an evening or two. It was breathtaking.

Just after eleven o'clock we watched one ship go northward over what looked like the next field. We saw another ship, which we thought at first to be a plane, come slightly southward toward the first one. They hovered together. Then we saw a third craft take off to our immediate left, over the trees bordering the field we were in. A few minutes later still another craft took off in a northerly direction. It moved over the trees next to the field. This craft made a noise. It sounded like a buzz, but not the familiar heavy airplane sound. It was almost a droning. The craft flew over our field and westward out of sight.

Then another ship rose up, also from the west, and crossed the street (Route 52) next to the hilltop where we were. The tree line was about half a mile from us, totally open to our view. The ship had a red flashing light and a white one, plus a set of red lights in a short row.

Suddenly it turned directly toward us, head on, and began brightening its starlight until it blinded us—at a distance of half a mile, no less! We had raised our cameras to snap some shots, and we clicked away. The UFO came closer and closer, and we had to shade our eyes because they were starting to hurt. My knees started to wobble, and I began to have second thoughts about whether I should run for cover. My heart was pounding in typical "fight or flight" response, but I remembered my vow and decided to fight by standing still and taking the consequences, if any.

I had to squint, even through the camera viewfinder. The ship suddenly turned from us and lowered its lights in one sweeping movement. To say we were nervous is an understatement. Harry said he was getting ready to grab me and run. I'd vowed never to flee but being in the situation is entirely different than thinking about it.

The ship simply continued on its way. For all I know the aliens were chuckling to themselves about how they'd scared the living daylights out of us to see what we were made of.

The following weekend we returned for another night of hunting UFOs in the country. We parked the car near a cornfield and walked up the road. A dirt tractor road we had missed as we drove around was now in front of us. The field adjacent to it was one of the larger fields in the area, about a quarter of a mile square. It was late August and the corn was as high as the proverbial elephant's eye, meaning about seven feet.

As we stood on the tractor road, I realized I was feeling something psychically or intuitively. Often when Harry and I walked into fields, I would tell him I felt a ship was nearby. He would say, "Come on, there's nothing here." We'd walk on and, sure enough, a ship would come by, although we never saw exactly where it came from.

When the moon was thin or absent, the fields were black. We couldn't see a thing. Other phases of the moon lighted the fields, and the contrast between full-moon and no-moon evenings was dramatic. This night the moon was nearly full. We remained on the dirt road for a few minutes, seeing nothing but cornstalks. Then I walked about twenty feet down the road. Harry didn't move. I said, "Harry, there's something here. I can feel it."

We stood still for several minutes more. Nothing was moving in the sky. After about five minutes of total silence and no activity, Harry said, "I'm going," and started to walk to the car. I stood there, frustrated. I felt something was going to happen and didn't want him to go too far without me. I started to walk after him but had taken only two steps or so when Harry turned around and yelled, "Oh, my God!"

I had my back to the cornfield. As I turned around, a ship silently lifted into the air with all its lights on. It had been sitting on the cornstalks a few feet from where I stood. It flew upward slowly but with obvious intent to avoid contact with me. It drifted over the field, moving away from us, flashing a small but bright white strobe light.

I screamed at Harry. "Damn it! I told you something was here! You never listen to me! I can feel when they're close by. . . ."

He was duly chagrined. "Okay, okay," he said. I took it for an apology. Then I yelled at the ship, "Why, why, why?" I could have reached out and knocked on its door. The aliens must have held their breath as we stood next to them.

We walked to where the craft had been. There was no damage at all to the corn where the ship had been sitting. It had rested on the stalks without placing any weight or pressure on them. I hate to use the cliché "antigravity," but the ship had essentially defied gravity in staying there silently and invisibly.

Our decision to enter the field and walk down the tractor road had been a last-minute choice. Apparently the ship was resting there, and the aliens felt our chances of bumping into it were remote. Or perhaps they wanted to see how clever we were. They obviously were avoiding one-on-one contact. They were staying just one step out of reach all the time, and they seemed to know us better than we knew ourselves. They seemed to know how we would probably react in most situations, and they relied on that knowledge to control the situations. We, like conditioned laboratory animals, came through with flying colors most of the time. It was beginning to look like a definite scientific field study, but the question was: who was conducting the study?

I didn't know exactly how and why I could feel the ships and the aliens. But that I did was a fact. I seemed to know exactly which fields to drag people into and when to move on. It was weird. Why was I so attuned to these beings?

Harry thought more about my "feelings" and emphasized his views on the psychic aspects to the UFO phenomenon. We got into battle after battle over this. Even though I'm psychic, I'm also a thick-headed skeptic who knows enough to check my perceptions, psychic or otherwise. I didn't know whether it was my own doing or whether something—or someone—was leading me. All I was sure of was that the ships were several steps ahead of us in this game. The only way I could see to catch them was through the element of surprise, which I continually used by driving along a road, stopping arbitrarily and running into a field. More often than not, ships were sitting there, and they had to take off to avoid unwanted contact.

To test the idea of taking them by surprise, I did something unusual that night while driving to another site. I slammed on the brakes. Even Harry wasn't prepared for it because if I'd said anything aloud, the aliens would have detected it. A ship with a flashing red strobe on it had been moving parallel to us along a treeline. It too was unprepared, and both Harry and I saw the back end of the craft actually rise up into the air, just like in cartoons when characters brake their vehicles really hard. It was comical but weird. I continued driving and then stopped short again. The ship did the same, all the while flashing its red strobe light. I have no idea why it was paralleling our activities.

But that insight into the element of surprise didn't resolve the dispute between Harry and me about whether my "feelings" were internally-generated psychic perceptions or were due to a sort of communication transmitted to me subliminally by the aliens—or had to do with something else. As I write this now, I believe that both possibilities were occurring.

Even though Harry and I didn't understand what was going on, it was clear we had no tangible proof that might help us to understand. All we could do was observe and take photographs—and I was the only one getting images on film. Harry never obtained any images on his film, even though he stood beside me aiming his twelve-hundred-dollar Leicas, one at a time, at the same ships I was photographing. We continuously tested his cameras and film by starting the evening with a photo of me while there was still some light outside. Those photos always looked fine in print. The rest of the roll was devoid of images. It was bizarre, baffling, and exasperating.

By October, I felt badly frustrated. Harry called his contacts around the country to see if someone would lend us equipment to capture evidence that would be of interest to the scientific community. One person sent us an infrared scope for night viewing. It turned out to be good only at a range of three feet or less for a burner of an electric stove set on ''high.'' In other words, useless.

One night, in desperation, I handed my Zenite to Sam and asked him to use it. I kept my Nikon and also had a super 8mm Bolex movie camera borrowed from my college. Harry had his two Leicas, making a total of five cameras among us. We liked to stand in a small, fenced-in Jewish cemetery on Route 52 because it was flat and treeless and offered a wide view of the sky. The fields around it were overgrown and couldn't be entered by foot, nor was there any gate except the entrance from the road. The cemetery is an area roughly one hundred feet by two hundred feet—perhaps half an acre in extent. We were, of course, respectful of the location.

As the three of us stood in the cemetery, nothing visible was flying. Sam said, ''Maybe we should meditate.''

I replied, ''You meditate, I'll watch the sky.'' Harry and Sam sat down on the ground. No sooner had they done so than, from across the street, large double headlights came sweeping up from the cornfield. I yelled, ''Here it comes!'' Harry and Sam jumped up. The craft turned toward us and crossed the road silently. It was so close to the ground that I could see it was lower than a nearby telephone pole.

Sam was closest to the craft. He yelled, ''It's got windows!''

Harry and I laughed and said, ''Sure, sure.'' The craft angled itself eastward so we could see an entire side as it slowly moved around the perimeter of the cemetery. There, as Sam had said, were three large, square windows about five feet by five feet in size. We could see into the craft to the top of the inside wall. It was lit with the same soft yellowish color as any electrically lit room used by humans would be. I was disappointed to notice that we couldn't see any computer-like equipment such as I had seen in California. In fact, we could see nothing except the wall. One spotlight shone under each of the three windows. The side of the craft was easily discernible, but we couldn't see the edges or ends of the craft. Beyond a few feet from the edges of the windows, the craft was obscured from our sight. That bothered me. I wanted to know why I couldn't see it completely. Seams and grooves on the metal were clearly visible. Various lights were visible on the exterior and they seemed bright enough that we should have been able to see its shape. I could tell the craft wasn't a triangular one. It appeared almost rectangular, but that was an educated guess. (Not until 1984 did I see the entire rectangle or boxcar shape of that type of spacecraft.)

The craft was visible for perhaps two minutes, then it flew eastward and was lost to sight beyond the tree line. As it passed around us, I filmed it while Sam and Harry clicked away with their cameras. I hoped the movie film would be revealing, but it proved to be a disappointment. It registered the dual headlights coming at us but not the windows. After the craft banked toward us, displaying its windows, the image on the movie film becomes one light bouncing all over the footage, frame after frame. Again, Harry got blanks. Sam's entire roll, however, registered some very unusual images, which I had to consider deeply before their true significance became apparent. Two sets of frame markings showed in each photo. Where each picture on a negative strip has frame marks or brackets separating each photo, it seemed the film had been "sprayed" *before* Sam started to photograph the ship, causing double images. Thus, when he took his first "real" set of photos, he was registering a second image on top of the first. The only way the film could have been sprayed is with radiation—shortwave radiation, to be specific.

This was my first major clue to understanding the UFO situation. Something or someone had used shortwave radiation to disturb the emulsion on Sam's film. I always believed that photographs would in time reveal a lot about the aliens and their craft. They were, in fact, to reveal more than I ever imagined and more than I even wanted to know.

I made a discovery one night that was to answer many of my questions and fill in many pieces of the UFO puzzle. On that night I watched a craft come down a hill as I stood in a field near a road. The craft skimmed along the ground and came toward me. I, in turn, ran toward it, thinking I could catch up to it. The craft got to the road, made a turn away from me, and vanished. It "appeared" to disappear.

I strained my eyes looking at the place where the craft should have been. All I saw was the road and the trees beyond it. Yet I felt sure the ship was still there. I stared at where the craft should have been, seeing nothing. I realized that all of our sightings had been of lighted craft. The only portions of the craft we ever saw were near lights on the craft—lights that were sometimes dim or barely visible, sometimes brilliant and blinding.

I discussed the situation with Harry. Suppose, I said, the metal of the craft was such that when unlit, it was rendered transparent or invisible, for all intents and purposes. We knew that even on our closest sightings, portions of the craft were invisible. Only lit portions were visible to us.

So many people seeing UFOs have reported that the craft "just vanished" or suddenly disappeared that the assumption developed among ufologists and the public at large that UFOs can dematerialize and must be "interdimensional" or "ultraphysical" or "metaterrestrial." A host of terms has been created over the years to describe the capability of UFOs to move in and out of our familiar three-dimensional space from other dimensions or space-times or, to use one of the most exotic terms, parallel universes.

I never accepted that theory. I still don't. If a person were looking at a fully lit UFO when it suddenly turned off all its lights, it would appear to vanish into thin air. But it would not have dematerialized; it would not be a psychic event. Its disappearance would be due to the operation of advanced technology—a kind of extraterrestrial "stealth" aircraft.

How does this technology work? The best explanation I can offer at this time involves an analogy to sunscreen glass used for eyeglass lenses. The glass is quite clear in darkness or low illumination, but when exposed to stronger light it gets darker until a pair of ordinary glasses becomes sunglasses. Similarly, the glass panes used in some contemporary buildings have a black appearance and are opaque when viewed from outside the building, but people inside the building can look out with almost no loss of visibility and not be seen. I speculate that the invisibility of UFOs is related. The metallic skin of a UFO probably has a molecular structure giving it properties similar to sunscreen glass. Under some conditions, controlled by electrical current, perhaps, it becomes opaque; under others it becomes clear to the point of transparency.

Another factor might be the color of the craft. Their silver color is akin to daylight. If, in addition, the craft's exterior has a fine grating or ridging all over—diffraction grating, to be technical—it would contribute to the invisibility by absorbing or diffusing light. A society that has developed the technology for UFO propulsion could also have developed metals, or possibly ceramics, with two states of visibility controlled by a craft's occupants. On the occasions I've been a few feet from craft, except for the instances when I saw windows with glasslike panes, the ships appeared solid, yet I presume the aliens must have had some means of observing the environment. In plain daylight, it is possible for ships to render themselves imperceptible. Going a step further, I've concluded that the ships fly as much during the day as at night, although their invisibility is more understandable at night.

Many questions about the UFO invisibility factor remain. I offer this speculation as a step toward scientifically understanding the situation.

My colleagues and I began to zero in on the aspect of

lit vs. unlit portions of the craft. We also watched airplanes, particularly during fuller phases of the moon. At those times, airplane shapes became quite clear, particularly when they flew in front of the moon. It was a different story with the UFOs. We never saw one pass in front of a full moon. On nights when we could clearly see airplane shapes, the ships were no more visible than any other time. Only the areas around their lights were visible.

On some occasions when ships turned off their lights within fifty feet or so of us, we couldn't see the metal. It was disconcerting to know that a UFO was there right in front of us yet invisible. We even had some sightings at dusk, when the sky was still light, in which a UFO stopped in the sky above us with one large light on—and that bright light was all we could see! One summer evening about six o'clock a craft came after us when we were driving. It ascended a bit and hovered over us, changing the strobe to a steady light. Even though it was daylight, we couldn't see anything but the area of the craft near the light.

This incident led us to think about all the sightings we had of fully visible ships. We realized that all the ships had a diffused glow around them. It wasn't a matter of seeing them fully because large lights were on. During one sighting—described earlier—seven of us watched a triangular craft pass silently over us in a twilight sky. The craft had a glow completely around it and two tiny round lights in the center of the underside. No other "normal" lights, such as headlights, were on. It was an incredible sight.

On another occasion Harry and I were at the bottom of Hill Avenue around one o'clock in the morning, en route to another site, when we saw the dual headlights of a craft coming toward us. I slowed down and it suddenly turned on a flat sheet of yellow lights on the underside, displaying its triangular shape clearly as it cruised by us, passing over the roofs of some nearby houses.

Our jaws dropped open. The underside of the triangle craft was a solid plate of yellow lights, but we could see seams in the metal under what looked like glass sheeting, indicating different-sized plates had been connected to form it. On numerous other occasions I've seen the underside of the triangle craft. With each encounter I've observed more and more details of the craft. The underside has looked the same each time but, interestingly, the right and left halves of the underside are not identical. Their seams are somewhat different, as I confirmed on later occasions.

I didn't take any pictures of the underside the first time because I was paralyzed by the awesome sight. Later, it bothered me that I didn't have the presence of mind to snap the shutter button. It annoyed me enough to prompt a call to an astronomer friend of mine at Montclair State College. I asked her whether she'd ever missed a rare photo opportunity, and she assured me that not only did it happen to her, it also happened to many astronomers who become startled or entranced at some beautiful meteor shower or other sky event. I was somewhat relieved after this conversation, and realized I couldn't do everything myself. This frustration led me into new avenues of exploration that proved successful in getting the ships on film hundreds of times.

# CHAPTER 6

• • •

# *PM MAGAZINE*
# GOES INTO THE FIELD

ABOUT THIS TIME, the Albany, New York, office of the well-known television program, *PM Magazine,* called *Omni* to find out whether anything notable was occurring with regard to UFOs. The call went to Harry, who described the nightly appearance of ships in Pine Bush and what we were doing there. The *PM Magazine* staff thought it would make an interesting segment. They wanted to meet us in Pine Bush in an attempt to get it all on videotape.

On Wednesday, October 1, Harry and I drove to Albany to meet one of the program's producers, Maribeth Carr, her associate producer, and their staff. We agreed to go to Pine Bush the following Saturday, where Maribeth and her people would have the necessary equipment to film a segment and scout the territory. Filming would actually be done on another day. The only condition we placed on Maribeth was not to bring extra people, neither staff nor friends. Harry and I wanted to keep the size of the group small to maintain some control over the situation.

Returning downstate on the New York State Thruway, my car had engine problems. Luckily, it happened directly across from the only gas station around for many miles. We had to take a Trailways bus home.

About 8:30 that evening, most people on the bus were asleep, including Harry. I gazed out the window at a sparkling-clear but very dark sky with many planes flying around. As we passed a grove of trees, a huge and intense red glow rose from the trees to follow the bus. I looked at it and realized it was a UFO. I woke up Harry and said, "Look, look!" He took one look and then exclaimed, "Holy shit!"

The craft looked like a glowing red diamond, unbelievably huge and very low. As I watched, it became obvious that the ship was out of the line of sight of the planes. It was below the trees, following the treeline about one-quarter of a mile away and could be seen only by those on the highway. For thirty minutes it paced us and then disappeared.

On Saturday, October 4, Harry and I met the *PM* group at McDonald's restaurant in Middletown, New York. The group consisted of Maribeth, her associate producer, Sharon, two camera/sound men and the girlfriend of one of them. As we walked outside to greet them, we saw Yvonne Comeau, Bob's daughter, with her boyfriend, Dean. Bob had told us about their encounter with a UFO while in a truck with her dog. Harry invited them to be part of the *PM* segment, and they agreed.

We reached the first site about seven o'clock in the evening. It was still light, and the sky was going to be marvelously clear. We walked to the crest of the hill and immediately some ships came toward us with red lights on. The *PM* people could see they weren't airplanes. Maribeth watched a craft change direction so abruptly that she was shocked. One ship had all its lights on, but it was too far away for any of us to photograph.

The ships were landing behind the nearest farmhouse, which belonged to a Crawford councilman. The cornstalks had prevented us from getting into the field once before, so we drove to the second site—Harry and I in my car and the others in their van with *PM Magazine* insignia on the sides. When we arrived, we could see craft flying around, circling the area with dim lights, often changing direction and coming in quite low, soundlessly.

After parking my car by the cemetery, Harry and I climbed into the van and we all drove down the dirt tractor road into the cornfield. Then everyone got out and looked up. There was so much activity that we all began to look at different things. Sharon stared at a stationary light that she thought was a bright star. The ''star'' suddenly shot across the sky and stopped. She was amazed and asked everyone repeatedly if they'd seen it.

I'd told her earlier about the frustration of one person seeing something that no one else saw, so I said, ''You see what I mean?'' I recalled the ''sky games'' I'd seen in California but had never seen in Pine Bush until now. It was interesting to know that the ships had a variety of consistent, if unpredictable, behaviors. In fact, the event Sharon had just witnessed led me to suspect much more was going on than we saw or knew about because the ships' activity had been so near but was so different from what I had previously seen in Pine Bush. Were there still other games in which the ships played with their audience?

I went to the trees at the end of the field to check if anything was parked on the ground, while the others stayed by the van. After about ten minutes of groping through corn and thickets of weed, I heard the others whistle for me to come back. I couldn't see anything moving, but nevertheless was annoyed at being recalled just when I was about to reach the place where I'd seen ships land many times before.

When I finally made it back to the van, the group asked me, ''Didn't you see what happened?'' They told me about two objects with red, unblinking lights, one atop the other, that had appeared in the sky just above and behind me. The objects seemed to be stationary and on either side of me. I hadn't seen them, which annoyed me further. The aliens had probably listened to me curse the vegetation that prevented my finding them.

We left the field and went to the Pine Bush Diner. The

*PM* insignia on the van, big and bright, was attracting attention—attention I didn't want. After having some food and filling up the van's gas tank, we returned to the second site. There wasn't much activity, however. The crew had brought video equipment to try filming the ships, but refused to do so, claiming they were too far away. I couldn't convince the cameraman even to try.

We called it quits about 12:30 A.M. and agreed to meet again in a week, but earlier in the day.

The following Saturday, with Sam along, we met at McDonald's at two o'clock in the afternoon and reached the fields an hour later. It was extremely windy, cold, and heavily overcast. The crew worked fast to set up because it was becoming too dark to film us in the fields.

As Harry, Sam, and I walked into the fields while the crew filmed us, I realized that Harry and Sam were wired for sound but I wasn't. I said to Maribeth, "Why don't I have a mike?"

Her reply astounded me. "We've decided that you're not going to be interviewed." My astonishment quickly turned to anger. After all, who was responsible for their being there in the first place?

I told Harry what Maribeth had said. He said something rivaling her for stupidity: "Just shut up and do as you're told." Sam overheard it all, intervened with Harry, and they both talked with Maribeth. She then said the crew hadn't brought enough videotape to interview me. I was beginning to steam.

We were filmed first while walking through the fields. Then interviews were to be shot. We'd arranged with Yvonne and Dean to tape them at Dean's house. As I drove there with Harry and Sam, followed by the van, it suddenly occurred to me that I held power because of my photos. Maribeth wanted to include them in the segment. So I said to Harry and Sam, "When we get to Dean's, tell Maribeth, 'Ellen says no interview, no pictures.'" They protested, but when we got to the house, they talked to Maribeth tactfully, and she gave in.

I suspected she was going to cut my interview later, and she did. Aside from a distant shot of Harry, Sam, and me walking through the field, there was only a shot of my face on screen for several seconds. Neither Harry nor Sam would say forthrightly what they thought was going on in Pine Bush. They skirted the matter, giving a watered down account loaded with disclaimers and tentative statements of what the three of us all knew we'd experienced. I was the only one who said directly, "in my opinion . . ." and that statement was cut from the segment along with the rest of my interview. I could see that the *PM* crew was beginning to have a bad attitude toward the whole affair, although I didn't know why.

Then the crew dropped a bomb on us. They'd decided they didn't want to say in the segment that they saw anything in the sky. All I could think was, "Of all the damn nerve!" They were afraid of ridicule, they said. The segment was carefully worded to state, ". . . on that particular night . . . we didn't see anything . . ." except for about a dozen UFOs!

The segment aired several times locally in 1981 and in August 1982 was shown on nationwide television.

Because of that experience and others, I've found people often have a delayed reaction after they see UFOs—a reaction characterized by fear and denial. I'll leave it to psychologists to explain. I found the way to get around this is to have a tape recorder continually recording when I'm out in the field with others. To date I have more than one hundred cassettes that constitute a record of the experiences I and others have undergone in pursuit of solution to the UFO mystery. I thought about having people who accompany me sign statements at the end of a trip to the fields, but that just isn't practical, and some people feel it is insulting as well. I've no wish to offend people, but it gets pretty offensive to me—as in the case of *PM Magazine*—

when my hard effort, pioneering work, original findings, and often spectacular sightings of UFOs are denied, avoided, ignored, or explained away by preposterous statements (not until 1987 would I receive serious media coverage). When will people learn not to fear the truth, but to fearlessly pursue it?

# CHAPTER 7

• • •

# OUT OF SIGHT, OUT OF PINE BUSH

BY THE MIDDLE of October, we noticed fewer ships in the sky. From July through September, we had seen as many as thirty lights in the sky at once, dancing around tree lines—and none of them airplanes. Now the activity consisted of only a few lights here and there at treetop level, although those few ships always came in close enough to let us see them clearly at least once a night.

By early November, we were worried. There seemed to be no ships anywhere. Once in a while we would see something above the trees, but these occasions were hardly worth talking about. Sam, who hadn't been along with Harry and me in several weeks, came up to Pine Push. We stood in a field and looked at the empty sky. Only an occasional airplane was flying. The stars were beautiful, but no ships were around.

I looked at my companions and said, "You see what the normal nighttime sky *should* look like. Only a couple of planes here and there, and that's it—not wall-to-wall flashing lights over us. Now what?" The UFOs hadn't told us where they were going, and I had a sinking feeling the game could be over.

It wasn't quite. On Thursday, December 11, I left my photography class about ten o'clock at night and began driving home. A UFO followed me from the Garden State

Parkway in Saddle Brook through Paramus, Hackensack, and into New Milford. I opened my window early on and said to it, "Come to my house." It was to do just that! As I turned onto my street, the craft came up the block with me, hovering just above the apartments that make up most of the large block where I live. I thought, "My God, it *is* coming to my house!"

I pulled into the driveway, jumped out of the car and charged into the house, yelling, "Mom, Dad. Come out here quick!" They both came running out. The craft, an intense white light, was hanging about five or six houses away, almost motionless except for a slight swaying movement. My mother took one look and said, "Oh, that's not a plane." There was no sound at all. The sky was bright and no planes were visible. I had no doubt that this was the same kind of triangle craft I had seen in Pine Bush.

The craft remained stationary for about twenty minutes. Then an airplane flew across our field of vision some miles away, apparently from Teterboro Airport. We could hear its roar and see the shape of its fuselage and wings. There was no comparison between it and the bright stationary light. When the plane was gone, the ship began to circle the area leisurely and did so for about two hours.

But that sighting was the last I had for quite a while. In the following weeks, Harry called around the country to learn what was going on. There were still plenty of sightings; the craft were still around. They just weren't where we were. Friends of mine insisted that Harry and I should go to the Wanaque Reservoir in Wanaque, New Jersey, where national headlines had been made in the 1960s when a UFO landed in the water. Police saw the craft come out of the water, and state officials had to investigate because the water was intended for human consumption. One officer was temporarily blinded by a light that shot out from the craft. Thousands of people came to the reservoir over the next few weeks, hoping to see UFOs. Finally, townspeople were fed up with the publicity and disruption. Floodlights were set up to illuminate the reservoir. The ships went away and so did the tourists.

I thought the Wanaque sightings were over, so it took some time to convince me to go there. Finally, one February night, I went. Harry came along. It was below freezing outside; the reservoir was iced over. I had brought my tripod and camera, just in case. I thought I'd try some time exposures. I'd never tried that before. But I really didn't expect to see anything.

We had obtained permission to enter the reservoir grounds. When we drove up to the gate and spoke with the guards, they said people, including guards and local police, were still seeing UFOs in the area. They gave us the name and telephone number of the officer who had been temporarily blinded by the craft coming out of the water during the original sightings.

We drove to the top of the dam, which gave us a fabulous view of the area. I set up my tripod and got back into the car. After about twenty minutes, a light suddenly rose from behind some small hills across the reservoir. It came right over the ice toward us and stopped midway across the reservoir. We could see portions of the craft but not the entire shape. A small red light bobbed randomly, and we realized it was dangling at the end of a wire or antenna projecting from the side of the craft.

The ship turned itself horizontally. It rotated 180° so that its opposite end was facing us. Whether this was its front or back, we couldn't tell. It looked as if several extensions protruded from the craft, all with small lights at the ends of them. They bobbed around the craft like a fishing pole bent from a weight on the end of its line.

I took several photos, including one five-minute time exposure. After about half an hour, the craft abruptly turned off all its lights, and we couldn't see it any more. When it became apparent that the UFO was gone, we drove back to the guardhouse and reported what we'd seen. The guards were astonished. And we had photographic proof. My time exposure turned out to be spectacular. (The Wanaque photograph appears in the photo section of chapter 16.) The other photos were unremarkable. We spent several more nights there but didn't see anything worth reporting. I suspected that the main sighting was only a fly-by and that the ships were not frequenting the reservoir any more.

Some of my close friends began sighting UFOs around New Jersey. One night in August, 1980, a girlfriend called me about nine o'clock to say she saw a ship in Tenafly, where she lived a few towns away. It was stationary above some trees, she said, and ''dangling things'' were coming out of it, along with strong beams of light. (She sounded very frightened. At first I thought she was kidding, but when she described certain details, I knew she was serious. She had planned to go to Pine Bush with me, but after this incident, she backed out.)

I raced over to Tenafly with my camera and saw a triangular craft cross a road to land behind some houses. For hours I tried to catch up with it. A lone hitchhiker also saw it when I stopped to question him. And as we were talking, a car with two girls stopped; they were also looking for it. As we stood there, we all saw the ship come across the sky again and dip below some trees.

I was becoming car sick from going around in circles. At one moment the craft would be over a house on the far side of a road or railroad track. I'd race across to get to it, only to find it gone. It would suddenly reappear where I'd just come from. I was also low on gas and no gas stations were open at that hour.

By two o'clock in the morning I was tired of getting nowhere and started to drive home. I realized the craft was about a block from me, following my car. As I crossed a railroad track, the UFO veered toward me, coming up to the side of my car. I stared at the triangular craft. It had the familiar black metal on parts of the front as well as the familiar starlight—the plus-sign-shaped light that looked as if each part of the plus-sign had been cut in half. The ship suddenly turned its starlight fully on and flashed it on-off, on-off. It veered away as I was coming to a stop across the tracks, giving me a good look at its aft section. That was the first time I got a good look at the back of a craft, and it surprised me. Although the craft was a triangle, the back seemed to have a sleekly curved hump that gradually flattened out to its pointed ends.

Returning to my house a bit shaken, I was nevertheless overjoyed at the interaction with whoever was flying the ship. The aliens had given me a "goodbye for the night" gesture, fully acknowledging my presence in a way that seemed to say they enjoyed it. It was still a "look but don't touch" game, but someone was having fun with me.

That experience was to be my last major encounter until 1984. I had a brief sighting one night in 1983 when I was driving, and for reasons I don't understand, it scared me. I heard of many sightings during that time, however, including some interesting encounters by some of my friends, none of whom knew that the others had had such an experience. I was becoming a UFO encounter coordinator, so to speak.

On September 12, 1982, the *Middletown Times–Herald Record* Sunday magazine section, *Sunday Record*, published a long article about UFO sightings in the area. I'll summarize it here, not because my experience is described—my July 18, 1980 sighting with Harry was highlighted—but because the full range of pro and con statements from local people was presented. It quoted the farmer I described in chapter 2 as a skeptic. Carl Balbach lives in Walden; he owns the field where Harry and I stood and has observed it daily since 1946. It is a cow pasture-hayfield that he mows twice a year. Moreover, his farmhouse windows look over the field so, he says, he can see what goes on there all the time. He told the *Sunday Record*, "I never saw anything; they [Harry and me] claimed to have, but I can't verify it one way or another. They made a big deal of it. I don't know these people, I can't vouch for them." I told Carl recently that he may be a native of the area, but mentally he's from Missouri, which is fine with me. I'm a skeptic, too. The difference is: I do the research.

The article noted that Harry and I had invited Carl to accompany us on our night vigils, but he never did. "They were up to all hours of the night. I have to get up at 4:30 to work. The last thing I want to do is sit up in a field, especially in the fall, to freeze my butt off." He added, "I can't say the man's a liar. He may have legitimately seen something."

I mention this statement in the interest of objectivity because, as the saying goes, lack of evidence is not evidence of lack. In this case, although Carl hadn't seen anything, lots of other people did. The article went on to describe the activities of UFO investigator Dennis Piaquadio of Newburgh, New York, a field investigator for the now-inactive National Investigations Committee on Aerial Phenomena (NICAP). Among the UFO cases he described, one was explained by him as either a hoax or a mistaken perception due to an ultralight, which is a hang glider with a motor attached. Another case, this time genuine, was a 1980 incident involving five New Windsor children ranging from nine to fifteen who saw a lighted object in the woods. One of them, a thirteen-year-old boy, described it as "triangular or diamond-shaped" with "mainly yellow and white lights around the edges." It was thirty or forty feet long and noiselessly swayed back and forth, he said, and was in view about twenty minutes. According to the mother of one of the children, it disappeared when they walked toward it, which terrified them. They came home in an incoherent state. Even animals were affected: her dog "went absolutely crazy, barking the whole night long." The next day she went with her children to the overgrown, swampy area where the object was sighted. She said she found an elliptical football-shaped area, 43.5 feet long, where "the weeds were flattened, white and totally devoid of any moisture."

She also reported finding several "bizarre footprints," 18.5 inches long and 8 inches wide at the broadest point. The imprint was about 1.5 inches deep; it showed one large toe and three small ones. "Whatever did it was very heavy," she concluded. (If this sounds like Bigfoot, you're right, as I'll discuss in the next chapter.)

I made periodic trips to Pine Bush to see what was happening, but nothing was going on. Soon thereafter, Harry moved to Florida. I was left alone in my effort to find financial and technical support for the research. I began to concentrate on interesting the media in what I was doing. A number of newspapers and magazines published articles. The Metaphysical Center of New Jersey, presided over by my friend Jean Munzer, proved enormously supportive in many ways.

But my main objective—unequivocal face-to-face contact with aliens and proof of it—eluded me; 1981 passed with no results and few sightings; 1982 and 1983 had no sightings for me, although one resident, Bob Lloyd, later told me the ships came back for two weeks in 1982. I was very weary and frustrated, but I knew enough about science to know that persistence is essential. I was determined. After making many trips to Pine Bush over a three-year period without seeing a single UFO, I arrived there in June of 1984 to find the sky filled with lighted ships. My mission was about to advance by a quantum leap.

# CHAPTER 8

• • •

# REENTRY: 1984

WHEN I REALIZED that evidence was in the mind of the beholder and since all I had brought away from my 1980 UFO experiences were photographs, I became determined to find professional people who would join me to obtain something tangible. I was open to almost anything else that offered promise of solving the UFO mystery, so when a medical friend suggested using kinesiology, one of his diagnostic techniques, to reach out to the ships, I agreed.

His method often proved successful in helping us zero in on the fields where we'd find ships and the timing for us to visit. I had my own sense of how to locate them, and we worked in concert. If we were driving about the area, I would tell him I thought we should, for example, make a right turn. He, in turn, would use his methods of channeling a higher source of knowledge to assess my calls. We were nearly always in agreement. Two results emerged: First, we had a number of close encounters; and second, my confidence in, and understanding of, my own ability deepened. I was so tuned in to the ships that I could almost smell them before I saw anything in the sky or on the ground.

Although my channeling colleague was very interested in the Pine Bush happenings, he had a medical practice to look after and soon found he couldn't continue our joint effort. Nevertheless, word circulated that I was looking for people to accompany me, especially scientists.

The size of the group accompanying me to Pine Bush began to grow. We found ourselves quite literally running through fields, chasing the ships. We learned the hard way that most fields have flat tractor roads and it wasn't necessary to climb through seven-foot-high cornstalks and rip our clothes on barbed wire. Many of the fields were inaccessible; they were too overgrown or too swampy or had six-foot barbed wire fences that were impossible to penetrate. We wore ourselves down trying everything to get to the ships, and I suppose that for a time we looked more like a comedy team than serious investigators. On the positive side, I was learning every bush, tree, and stream in every field.

I also noticed something else: The ships' behavior was somewhat different toward me and those with me than it was in 1980. My photographs were also markedly different. I was still finding images of things we didn't see, but a new feature appeared in them—a large, round, opaque "globe" seemingly as large as a house, sitting on the ground looking as if it were just resting on the corn. Coincidentally, I added the element of flash to my photos so that foreground could be seen—foliage, fences, and so forth—and I would have a reference point if the sky was visible. That addition proved to be a tremendous aid for study of the images.

At first I had no idea what the strange globe was. A younger friend of mine, Cathy McCartney, began to go to Pine Bush with me regularly. She also had a Nikon camera and after many trips there during which many photographs were taken, a story began to emerge, which is told in chapter 11.

My various colleagues and I experienced the incidents ranging from many lights doing all sorts of angled turns in the sky to clear views of ships taking off and landing in many farm fields. Something was leading me. Although the aliens had always seemed playful rather than hostile, a number of experiences were to prove hair-raising and, upon reflection, enlightening.

One evening my friend Eleanor Motichka and I went to the Jewish cemetery to watch for ships. After leaving the car parked outside, we squeezed through the gate, and walked into the cemetery to look around at the fields and sky. We stood there, watching and talking, telling jokes and laughing even more at the thought of the aliens taking notes on the jokes. After about half an hour I heard a rustling in the bushes past the cemetery fence on the west side, where thick forest borders it. Glancing at Eleanor, I realized she didn't hear it. I was accustomed to having my senses heightened when out in the fields, regardless of what I was doing, and little went by me unnoticed. I didn't say anything to Eleanor, knowing she would be frightened.

Suddenly, there was a louder noise, as if someone kicked a branch. Eleanor heard it. "What's that?" she whispered loudly.

I told her it was probably an animal. Actually, in all the years I'd gone into the fields and woods of Pine Bush, I never ran into another person nor had I run into any animals that appeared dangerous except for a few house dogs who chased cars. So it was a surprise to hear noises in the woods, especially just beyond the cemetery fence.

We stood frozen, listening for more sounds. Eleanor said, "Let's go."

I said, "Wait a minute . . ." in a loud voice. "I'm not moving. . . ." The sharp sound of a large branch being broken in two pierced the air, followed by footsteps. We gasped. Eleanor exclaimed, "Someone's there! Let's get out of here."

I thought about it for a moment. No one could possibly be in the woods. We would have heard them walking through, and they would have seen us. Besides, the woods were too thick and overgrown for anyone to walk in at night. It had to be a ship. I said, "Shhhh! Don't move." We stood still, our hearts pounding.

Then, in a semi-loud voice, I repeated, "I'm not moving. If there's a ship in there, I want to see it." With that, "someone" picked up a good-sized rock and smashed it to the ground.

Eleanor and I nearly jumped out of our skins. She yelled, "Let's go!" To get back to our car, however, we had to squeeze through the slight opening between the gate and fence that is closest to the woods where the sounds came from. My knees started to buckle from fear, but I was determined not to let terror overcome me as it had in my 1980 close encounter. Reaching the locked car, I fumbled with my keys before we could get inside. I suppose my trembling slowed up things a bit also. But we finally got into the car and started laughing hysterically—not that anything was funny, but we must have looked like a comedy act.

Eleanor said, "Turn the car on. We have to get out of here." "No way," I said. "A ship is in there and I want to see it."

But she insisted, so I started the engine and slowly backed up, shining the headlights into the woods and stopping to look. Then I backed up the car on the roadside next to woods. Suddenly, all the lights of a triangle craft came on as it lifted up out of a small clearing between the trees, not twenty feet from the cemetery fence. My tape recording of that evening shows I gasped, "Oh, my God!"

Eleanor and I discussed the event many times, and in replaying it, we decided the ship must have been in the woods when we pulled up and walked into the cemetery. The aliens heard us and probably thought we would leave soon. When we didn't, delaying their departure, they used an elementary ploy to chase us away: fear. And when their first sound didn't work because I caught on to what was happening, they slammed a large rock at the ground, letting us know definitely that someone was there. It was simple, and it worked, to my dismay. That night has nevertheless been one of the highlights of my Pine Bush adventure.

The ships were in full swing throughout 1984 and 1985.

I took a carload of people with me every time I went—just about anyone who wanted to go. Most people saw lights doing wild things in the sky. On a few occasions, people came with a negative attitude and felt we were going up there to be abducted. When the ships moved away from us and no abduction occurred, I realized that I shouldn't take such people with me any more. I wasn't obligated to take anyone; they could go on their own if they want to. However, only I had obtained permission to go on people's property, so others would have to stick to the road if they didn't accompany me.

Sometime in 1984, I met Dr. Hans Holzer, an internationally known parapsychologist. It was a most fortunate meeting, as he put me in touch with two people who would radically enlarge my understanding of what the ships and their occupants were all about.

The woman called me one day. I didn't know anything about her; Dr. Holzer hadn't told me he was sending her my way. She talked guardedly about UFOs and I responded with caution. But I was curious because she seemed knowledgeable and mentioned details about the ships that I thought no one else knew.

For an hour we played the game of twenty questions, neither of us wanting to say too much, but each of us intrigued with the other. When I told her I had about 150 photographs of the ships taken in Pine Bush, she decided she wanted to visit me and see my work.

Her name was Dale. She and her colleague, Mark, came to my home one evening a few days later. My mother was present. Since I'd begun showing my photographs to people five years earlier, I'd always had to explain the details. I even used tracings to highlight details because I knew what I had on film was difficult to accept. Yet for all my efforts, the level of understanding I had seemed less than satisfying. I had taken the photographs, but I didn't truly comprehend them. All that was to change.

Dale and Mark told me they had worked together in the

Boulder, Colorado, area several years before, doing exactly what I was doing in Pine Bush—photographing and cataloging UFOs for a government study. I never learned what Mark's precise role or duty was—he didn't say and I didn't ask—but Dale was in the medical field, called in to examine the hundreds of cattle and other animals that were being mutilated through surgical techniques. I was doubly astounded. First, I'd known about the mutilations but didn't understand the situation. (For a good summary, see *Mute Evidence* by Daniel Kagan and Ian Summers.) Second, the government was paralleling my own work and, by Dale and Mark's account, was not so far ahead of me.

They told me further that they'd observed directly that UFOs were responsible for the livestock mutilations—mutilations that are still occurring today. Cattle blood, it seems, is closer in chemical composition to human blood than any other animal's, even though we appear physiologically closer to the anthropoids than the bovines. Exactly what the blood was being used for by the aliens, they didn't know. In light of Budd Hopkins's *Intruders* and the genetic experiments he hypothesizes, one could guess it was unhealthy for humans. As for the photography, the only difference between what the government and I were doing was this: the government effort drew upon vast resources of scientists, technicians, and equipment with sufficient funds to collect data in a concerted, comprehensive manner. This was slightly different from my own approach. . . .

I showed Dale and Mark my photographs. When they turned to the two photographs of the five aliens, which I discuss in chapter 16, they picked out all the figures immediately. In fact, they needed no help in understanding any of my photographs. My mother and I glanced at each other in amazement. When they turned to the photo of the large globe sitting on the ground, they both said, "Uh oh. . . . This picture is going to get you into trouble later."

I told them I had photographed some other less spectacular globes but didn't understand the pictures. They said the globes were "Tesla fields," named for the scientific genius Nikola Tesla, whose electrical research in the late nineteenth and early twentieth centuries is more responsible for the age of electricity and, later, the age of electronics than the far better known Thomas Edison. It was Tesla who made possible the long-distance transmission of electricity by creating the rotating magnetic field that allowed alternating current to be harnessed. It was Tesla who envisioned factories run by electricity. It was Tesla who created the induction motor, neon and fluorescent lights, wireless transmission of power, the laser beam, and hundreds of other brilliant inventions. *Tesla, Man Out of Time* by Margaret Cheney gives a good overview of the man and his work.

However, much more needs to be said, especially about his "reality engineering" in the form of electrogravities, the higher-order dimensions underlying the three-dimensional world we commonly experience as reality. Tesla's pioneering research in this area, according to physicist and former Army intelligence officer Thomas E. Bearden and others, gave the Soviet Union access to the technology underlying what is called psychotronics, a breakthrough in science based on mind-machine interface devices. The Soviet Union has apparently used its knowledge to manufacture psychotronic weapons, a generation of war machines beyond nuclear devices, according to syndicated columnist Jack Anderson, who reported on it first in early 1981, with followup columns in 1984. Tesla's insights into the nature of electromagnetism and the other forces of nature lead directly to UFO propulsion systems, Bearden and other psychotronic researchers say. Bearden shows that antigravity devices and free energy or fuelless generators are possible, along with thought transference, through a deeper understanding of electromagnetism first indicated by Tesla. In Bearden's 1980 book, *The Excalibur Briefing,* and various articles published since then, he has laid out the theoretical basis for what can be called UFO propulsion, surveillance, and communication systems. Also, following

Tesla, he calls for a fundamental revision of electromagnetic theory and provides the physics and math to back up his call. His 1988 book, *Aids—Biological Warfare,* published by the Tesla Book Company in Greenville, Texas, has a full description and graphic depiction of Tesla fields. Another basic text on psychotronics is John White's 1988 anthology, *Psychic Warfare—Fact or Fiction?*

When Dale and·Mark introduced me to Tesla's work, it was the first time I'd heard the term "psychotronics." The theory of the Tesla field is a byproduct of Tesla's investigation into fundamental forces of the universe. It can be set up to act as a shield or umbrella, around an object, or even something as large as a city, and thus has military applications in defending civilians from incoming missiles—apparently one of the uses the Soviets allegedly have made of psychotronics. Dale and Mark said the government realized that the aliens had psychotronic technology and that it was also experimenting with psychotronic devices to reproduce Tesla fields itself.

I asked Dale and Mark why I had "extra ears" on my telephone line. I'd begun to have disturbance on incoming and outgoing phone calls, and on several occasions I was disconnected a number of times during a single phone call, just as the conversation got down to the nitty-gritty about my UFO research.

They said to be thankful it was only on the phone, rather than someone knocking on my door. I didn't like that at all. I'm straightforward, sometimes disturbingly so to some people, without pussyfooting around. I didn't think I had anything to hide, yet no one was financing my research, and I was barely scraping by from week to week on my earnings as a word processor for a temporary employment service. What Dale and Mark said angered rather than scared me.

But I wasn't mad at them. Actually, we hit it off as friends. The meeting ended with an agreement to go to Pine Bush.

Dale and Mark had also said there was a terribly malevolent aspect to the aliens. I knew the ships were not here
to save the world, as so many people believed. But I had
never felt they were harmful in any manner. In fact, I had
received the opposite impression. As I mentioned in chapter
4, soon after my Pine Bush experiences began, I had felt
love for the ships and their occupants, which surprised me.
Now I was being told they were not so wonderful, were,
in fact, far from it.

None of my encounters had ever been bad, however. I
had no indication of hostility or danger, yet I had always
felt something was terribly wrong with the situation. People
were ''earmarked,'' zeroed in on and left to deal with close
encounters on their own, which usually involved ridicule
and confusion, if not terror that left them deeply traumatized. People's lives had been profoundly disturbed, entirely
against their will. This was not sweetness and light from
Space Brothers here to prevent the planet from destruction.
What was going on? Why the mixed signals or conflicting
perceptions of what the aliens were all about?

The first night Dale came to Pine Bush, Mark was unable
to accompany her. She brought another friend, Joe, and I
introduced them to Bob Lloyd, a former Wallkill resident
(now deceased) who had been abducted in the 1960s. I had
been put in touch with Bob through Butch Hunt, the town
barber. We quickly got into a deep discussion about the
UFO experience and began to flesh out a picture of what
seemed to be happening. I didn't agree with all that was
said but most of it made sense to me. We all agreed, however, that something monumental was occurring that would
probably affect everyone on the planet sooner or later, and
that the experience definitely had a negative side.

Judging from my photographs alone, I agreed with Dale
and the others that there seemed to be many races of alien
beings involved, since I could see five distinctly different
kinds in my pictures. Their mission was not to play with
us. That seemed merely a distraction for them, perhaps un-

dertaken to cut down the boredom while waiting for the important action to be accomplished. But what was the real mission?

Bob's twenty-year-old daughter had never seen the ships. She accompanied us that evening when we went into the field for more observations. We decided to go to the cemetery.

When we arrived there, lights were flying all around the area. A large lit object came up from the trees toward us. Bob had brought his video camera, but it was in the car. The object cast a fabulous shadow on the house next to the cemetery as it approached us. This happened rather quickly. I noticed the object coming toward us and yelled, "Look at what's coming!"

They all said, "Yeah, yeah . . . ," but no one moved.

I raced around the cemetery fence and cut through bushes to get into the field. The entire lighting system changed, and a hulk of a triangle ship came to the cemetery fence, entirely lit and completely silent. It was about sixty feet on each side, with antennalike projections bobbing from it. I could clearly see every seam and detail. It came up to the far side of the cemetery, within twenty feet or so of where I stood, then stopped briefly and simply reversed direction, slowly heading back to where it came from. The reversal without turning was staggering to watch. I could see every groove in the ship's metal exterior. A discharge or mist seemed to surround it, almost as if faint electrical currents were bouncing around its outside.

As it moved away, I noticed a rustling sound. It was the others coming into the field to join me.

I questioned them. "Why didn't you come into this field with me? Bob, why was your video camera in the car instead of in your hand?"

The conversation that followed raised some eyebrows. One of the four said he received a distinct mental message to stay exactly where we were. I, on the other hand, received a mental message to "go for it," which I did. My companion's message was quite clear: don't move. Mine was totally different in meaning. Someone or something wanted me to get close to the ship. Why, I asked myself.

We walked along the fence to its end, where the field opened out. Joe happened to look down and said, "What the . . . Look down."

There in the ground was a perfectly oval depression, about three feet across and eight inches deep, exactly like the ones Harry and I had found the day after our first sighting in 1980. The ground was pressed inward from something that obviously was very heavy and shaped like a giant egg. No grass of any kind was inside it—just dirt—and the surrounding weeds actually defined the marking. It was one of four pod marks we were to find. I started thinking about the events leading up to this event.

The night before, I had been across the street with Cathy McCartney and a friend of hers. We were deep in the cornfield across from the cemetery, where we found a dead and partially decayed deer that didn't look like it was undergoing natural decomposition. It had no blood that we could see; no flies were around it and no maggots in it. While we were there, Cathy, her friend, and I saw a UFO take off from the field where we were now standing, in back of the cemetery. We had been across the street, too far into the field to run out after the craft, but it looked as if it had been directly behind the cemetery, where the group and I now stood observing the depression.

Dale had come along with me because I had told her about the dead deer and she, having a medical background, and experience examining livestock mutilations, wanted to look at it. As we stood around the depression/pod mark, Dale said, "Look for a second pod depression down the fence line. There should also be a shallower depression between the two from another pod balancing the weight of the craft." Sure enough, we found them as she said. The two deep pod marks were about thirty-five feet apart. The three pod marks were all the same size and shape. Only the depth differed; the center pod mark wasn't as deep as the other two.

Then Dale said, "The front pod should have the gook in it."

"What gook?," I asked.

"The residue from one of the energy sources is released into the front pod," was her astounding reply.

We walked toward what apparently was the mark from the craft's front pod. In the depression was a strange-looking grayish substance. It seemed like cotton candy or spider webs. Dale called it gook, I called it gunk.

I asked, "Now what do we do?"

"About what?" Dale asked.

I said, "If you think I'm going to leave the gunk here, you're mistaken. I want to have it analyzed somewhere."

"You can't just pick it up. It's irradiated."

We all looked at each other. Joe picked up a stick and pushed the substance around in the pod mark. I photographed the marks. "So now what?" I asked. "Everyone wants evidence, we have it here, and we can't move it."

I felt uncertain, and so I deferred to Dale's judgment. She explained that it was highly contaminated. In retrospect, I think it was one of the biggest mistakes I've made. I now deeply regret not collecting samples, nor calling the police to come and see the pod marks and gunk. But I had no means for handling what Dale said was radioactive material.

We started talking about the details on the craft, reveling in the glory of such a spectacular sighting. I said to Bob, "Well, how could we have missed on an incredible sighting when in a group of five, two of us have seen aliens?"

Dale said, "Three." We all looked at her.

"You've seen aliens?" I exclaimed.

She said, "Honey, I haven't even begun to tell you what went on out West. . . ."

Bob and his daughter left. The girl, normally talkative, didn't say a single word after the sighting. She was simply staggered. Days later, Bob said, she was still silent and awed by it.

Dale, Joe, and I sat in the car by the cemetery gate. Lights were still flying around the tree lines. I'd found that Dale didn't like to give direct answers to questions. She sometimes would evade me if I approached her head-on in conversation. But if I let her talk, she would usually get around to my questions, and then the response was very satisfying because she obviously knew so much.

So we sat in the car and I let her do the talking. She told us that she and Mark realized early on that they weren't being told the full story of what the government wanted to do about the aliens. So they would go wandering around on government land, crawling over or under barbed wire. Apparently the aliens wanted a specific farm. The government somehow displaced the owners and then moved in with equipment. Dale and Mark wanted to find out what they weren't being told but were sure was going on. Sometimes they were caught and forced to leave the area, but they persisted in order to get at the truth about UFOs.

As Dale rambled on, she warned me to watch out when walking through the woods because in it were things that didn't belong. "What kind of things?" I asked.

"Animals that are not indigenous to an area," she said.

Immediately I recalled an incident one night when Eleanor and I had driven slowly along a road in Pine Bush. My headlights shone on an animal in the middle of the road, sitting on the yellow line. I slowed down to look at it, thinking it was a raccoon. But as we got close to it, I saw it wasn't that at all. It was a lemur! I couldn't believe my eyes. A lemur, a monkey from the jungles of Madagascar, was right there in Pine Bush. There was no mistake. We saw it up close and in detail, especially its round eyes and tail. It stayed there as we slowly drove past.

I said, "Eleanor, tell me that wasn't a monkey."

She replied, "Sorry, but we just saw a monkey in the road."

The following day I called my sister, who is a former environmentalist for the United States government, a ten-year veteran, to ask why a lemur would be on the road in Pine Bush. She had no answer. Neither did I, and I couldn't get over the image I'd seen.

So when Dale said there were other things in the woods, I said, "Like lemurs?" Her mouth dropped open as she turned around to look at me. I told her the story. She said the lemurs were the harmless ones. There were other animals that weren't harmless, such as Bigfoot and something called Mothman. She knew I didn't believe everything she told me, but I always kept an open mind and let her talk without making any remarks. In time, I learned she never lied. She knew about too many things that I had also seen for me to doubt that she was on the level.

Some time later I spoke with several hunters who also had seen lemurs in the woods around Pine Bush. One of them was Bob Lloyd. I was telling him what Dale had said about "unearthly" animals, and it prompted him to relate that he and a friend had seen a lemur. Like me, he never forgot the image of it. In *The Andreasson Affair*, Betty Andreasson recalls seeing lemurs during her abduction in the rooms where she was taken aboard the craft. Are the lemurs from this planet or the aliens'? Were they in a laboratory and then released? Did they just escape?

The release of out-of-place animal life into the woods of New York State is unsettling, to say the least. It is absolutely frightening when you hear stories about the encounters people have had with creatures that simply should not be here on earth, let alone in the Pine Bush area. One resident told me that while he was hunting, he was chased by something invisible. He heard it clearly and it smelled rotten. The man's dog ran out of the woods and back to the house. The man also ran, holding his rifle, and ended up in a tree. Whatever it was, when it got to the base of the tree, it apparently couldn't climb. After a while, it went away. He, who had been hunting those woods since he was a boy, was very frightened by the incident. The man also described some of the things Dale had told me took place in Colorado. Since he didn't know Dale, it felt very eerie to hear almost identical details.

Spring passed into summer, and each week I'd hit the road for Pine Bush with an entourage of various people. We had many sightings that, technically speaking, were close encounters (CE) of the first kind—i.e., a UFO in close proximity (within five hundred feet) of the witness. We allowed some close encounters of the second kind—i.e., a CE that influences the environment in some fashion, usually by leaving physical evidence of its presence or creating electromagnetic interference. In our case, it was crushed vegetation and landing pod marks. But as interesting as the CE1s and CE2s were, to my disappointment we had no CE3s—close encounters of the third kind in which occupants or entities are associated with the sighting. (As for close encounters of the fourth and fifth kinds—communication with aliens and abduction by aliens, respectively—see chapter 14.)

The end of 1985 was marked by several incredible sightings and incidents that "blew my mind." In December, three women friends and I were in one of the farm fields when a large craft came up from a field several tree lines away. It moved toward us with dangling antennae on the sides and front. It crossed the field next to us, lower than tree height, curved around us and stopped in midair. We stared at it. I had my tape recorder on throughout so I could describe what was going on.

As we stood there, it seemed the ship shifted to another mode of power. It started to rumble and increase its noise level. The ground shook beneath us and the noise was like thunder bouncing off the hillsides, echoing and reverberating in the valleys all around.

I continued talking into my tape recorder over the sound of the ship. One of the women, Joan, said, "Air booms. Doesn't that sound like an air boom?"

We looked at each other. Air booms along the East Coast have been occurring for hundreds of years. The official explanation is that they're due to airplanes breaking the sound barrier, but that explanation doesn't account for reports of air booms from as early as the 1700s. Could UFOs be responsible for them? Have they been around that long? Here, before our eyes, was an undeniable example of a ship demonstrating what power it really had and how it could produce the phenomenon. I also felt for the first time that the ship was making a show of power to demonstrate what it was capable of doing. Playtime was over.

# CHAPTER 9

• • •

# ALIENS UNDERGROUND

DURING THE SUMMER of 1985, people accompanying me to Pine Bush and I sometimes saw flashes of light from various fields for hours on end. We didn't pay much attention to them for some weeks. After all, we were there to see lights in the sky, not the ground. Moreover, at ground level we couldn't see the source of the distant flashes through the vegetation. In time, however, we were to be staggered by the realization that the *aliens were constructing underground installations*.

At first we thought someone must be working in the fields. That explanation seemed slightly ridiculous because it was the middle of the night and there were no sounds of heavy machinery, but we simply didn't think much about it or immediately suspect anything. We did check it out to the extent of calling a number of authorities to ask whether they could account for the activity. We were told they knew of nothing.

We also thought it might be heat lightning. But it soon became obvious that the constant flashes were not weather-related because one hot night we saw real heat lightning and knew unmistakably that it was different from what we were seeing from the fields. On another occasion an air traffic controller living nearby came along with me after his shift and saw the end of the light show. He took one look and said, "No way is that heat lightning."

It was becoming obvious the aliens were involved, so one night about two months into this light show a group of us decided to find higher ground in order to watch the flashes better. When we climbed a hill to get a clearer view, we began to feel uneasy. Looking into one of the larger fields no more than a mile away, we could see lights coming from the ground. Some of them looked huge, like arc lights used for piercing the sky to call attention to the grand opening of a store or to a movie premiere. Others looked more like laser beams. The astounding thing was this: the upward-shining lights actually *bent around in a curve* until they circled back toward the ground like a rainbow.

We tried to get into the fields where the activity was going on. Every time we drove toward one of the lighted fields, it went dark. We could look down into the fields from various high points, but it seemed we were not "invited" to view them at closer range. It was as if the activity was of incredible importance and no alien would allow the field's security to be breached.

What was going on? When we checked the fields the next day, we saw no evidence of mining. Occasionally, some of the local residents found diggings on their property—diggings large enough to have been made by machinery—but where no construction had been authorized by the owners. All the land is privately owned by farmers, who plow and plant. Some ground markings were here and there, but it was as if whatever occurred at night was removed or camouflaged against curious people like us.

So what caused the diggings, we wondered. Here was a mystery for which I discerned the vague shape of an answer, but it took a startling incident to make it perfectly clear.

One night I was on a dirt road beside a field far in back of the Jewish cemetery with part of a New Jersey family, the Schappers, and a couple of other people. After standing on the road for half an hour, I felt we ought to walk into the field. We went toward a fence, and suddenly we were blasted in the face by a loud noise like a helicopter. We hit the ground quickly, then looked up, thinking something was coming down on us. Nothing was there, yet the noise continued. We had to scream at each other to be heard.

I yelled, "It's in front of us!"

"It" was in front of us yet we couldn't see it. The sound lifted off the ground and moved away. A ship apparently had been sitting right there. It must have been doing something and had counted on us not getting to it before it finished.

The aliens must have misjudged our actions and thought they would blast us with noise to stop us until their ship was airborne and away from us. The noise sounded as if it were a helicopter with unlubricated rotor bearings—steel grinding steel—right next to us.

We returned to the cemetery. The craft came back over the field and crisscrossed it from side to side. Someone said, "What the heck is it doing?"

We watched it for a few minutes, trying to figure out its behavior. Suddenly, I realized what was happening. The craft was moving in a search-and-rescue pattern. It must have left in such a hurry that the aliens decided to make sure they hadn't left anything behind. I was sorry we left the field so quickly. If the ship had left something, it would have been one hell of a find.

But apparently it hadn't. It left and so did we. Some nights we heard loud drilling sounds coming from the woods. We heard what seemed to be generators and motors running. One night, a local resident went out on his own to try to find where the sound was coming from. He couldn't. No matter which direction he walked in, he told me later, the noise seemed to come from another.

Dale and her husband, Dave, came up to Pine Bush. I still had no clear sense of exactly what the ships were doing there. I was about to find out.

The three of us walked behind the cemetery. All of a

sudden, we were blasted by air from the ground, like being caught in a windstorm. I screamed, "What's happening?"

"Wait a minute and it will stop," Dale yelled. It did.

She and her husband started stamping their feet into the grass. "What the heck are you doing?" I demanded.

Dave shouted, "That was warm, dry air."

I said, "So . . . ?"

Dale shouted, "Don't you get it?"

"No."

They both yelled at me, "Generated air . . . as in artificially produced air . . . as in air being released from a structure of some kind."

I was confused. I said, "Are you telling me there's something underneath here and we were just blasted by air from a vent?"

They both yelled, "Hurray! Now you're getting it!"

To say I was dumbfounded would be an understatement. Dale had told me nothing about this before. She wanted to wait until I found out for myself, knowing full well I wouldn't believe her if she had told me.

The aliens apparently were building underground structures all over and Dale had had plenty of previous experiences with them out West. The air venting took place in the flat fields through some kind of piping (that we couldn't find). The venting was moved around the field so that a person wouldn't get blasted by the airstream more than once at the same spot and would probably just dismiss the event as a natural atmospheric phenomenon, like dust devils. I had accidentally been in the right spot at the right time. Moreover, I was fortunate to be with someone who understood what was going on and could explain it.

If the venting was in the fields, I thought, and structures really were hidden beneath the fields, where would the entrances be? It took perhaps two seconds to figure out they would be in the woods. I said, "Oh, my God."

"What's the matter?" Dale asked.

"If you tell me the entrances are in the woods, I'm going to scream."

"Not only the woods, but in all the mines that have been closed down."

Everything fell into place. Until then, I hadn't figured out why the ships were landing in the same fields and forest areas night after night. The ships were always in the woods, in exactly the same place month after month, year after year, but we still couldn't get to them. The terrain was too rough. The drilling was in the woods—in the middle of the night, no less. I'd been there with other people, and we'd heard it. But we couldn't find its source. The noise seemed to be everywhere we walked. Now the reason was clear: it was coming from under us.

I said to Dale and her husband, "Would you tell me what in hell is going on?"

They told me a story about the earth being up for grabs by many extraterrestrial races who have come to claim a stake.

I thought they were off their rockers. I still don't believe their story, but I'll save my own beliefs on the matter for chapter 17. I wanted to find the entrances in the woods. I presumed they would be well covered or camouflaged, in addition to being relatively inaccessible because of the dense forest cover. Thus, I figured, the entrances wouldn't be portable like the vents, giving me time to attempt to find them. I dropped the urgency I'd first felt about finding them and thought about the easier portions of my quest. Nevertheless, I began to spread the word to friends, colleagues, and other UFO researchers that I thought the aliens were building underground structures.

To find the entrances, I'd have to comb the woods during the daytime. Yet I also had to have an income because no one was funding me to do research. I couldn't be there night and day. I would need help, but it was difficult enough getting people to come to Pine Bush for a night. How could I get them to donate their daytime also?

And would I know an entrance if I found it? What do they look like? The search would be like seeking an invisible needle in a gigantic haystack.

I told Dale I wanted to look for the entrances. She said to me, "Don't you think these entrances are guarded?"

"By what?" I asked.

"What do you think wildlife such as Bigfoot is for?"

"Oh, no! You're not going to lay that on me. . . ."

"You don't have to believe me," she said. "I'm just telling you to beware."

Just what I needed to hear! But now, several years later, I've been through the woods many times, day and night. So have some colleagues. We can't find the entrances. The areas to be covered are too vast. It would be sheer luck to stumble onto something—or deliberate manipulation by the aliens.

For example, one night I accidentally passed a field where drilling was occurring about midnight; no lights were being used, of course. The drilling was so loud that I heard it with my windows rolled up and the air conditioning on. I almost thought the noise was coming from the transformer on a utility pole I was passing.

But something clicked in my mind. I pulled over and opened my window. I clearly heard something like a pneumatic drill from the dense forest behind a small field. I got out of my car with my flashlight and crossed the brushy border into the field. It was eleven o'clock. I was alone and afraid in the dark, but determined, even as my knees began to shake.

I kneeled and stupidly shined my flashlight into the woods. The drilling stopped. I held my breath. Nothing happened. For an hour I sat on the ground without moving, but I heard nothing more. The meaning was clear: I was not welcome to observe their operations, let alone their installations.

And what are the installations for? Laboratories? Some abductees have described being led into large areas with many rooms; that would fit the bill exactly. We also believe that aircraft are being housed in these installations. On many occasions we have seen ships come down to ground level and not rise for the rest of the night. On other occasions, at dusk we have seen ships ascending from the ground in the areas we suspect have the entrances (although we recognize they could have landed invisibly).

I'm not alone in my conclusion that there are underground alien bases. I have received reports from around the country about underground drilling in woods during the night and electrical generators operating in areas where no one is doing construction. In fact, the *National Enquirer* ran a headline story about an alien base at Dulce, New Mexico, saying it was jointly staffed by aliens and the CIA. The alleged source of the information, Leonard Stringfield, is a respected ufologist, and he protested that story was based on comments he made in a public lecture where he simply reported what another person had claimed. That person was John Lear, a commercial pilot and test pilot who lives in Las Vegas, Nevada. Stringfield himself neither endorses nor denies the idea of alien bases. Lear, however, claims there are many alien bases—Groom Lake, Nevada, is another site he names—that are being linked through mining operations coast to coast. He claims the aliens are malevolent and are the cause of animal mutilations and even some human mutilations among their numerous abductions.

I have no information bearing on Lear's claim. But if underground installations are being used to house alien aircraft, as I have concluded, there must be a large number of such aircraft already there. I think a person would feel the ground rumble when an entrance opens nearby. One hunter told me that he'd felt precisely that on several occasions in a certain section of forest, and on each occasion, animals fled the area. He took his cue from them and also left. I feel we are closing in on the aliens and it's only a matter of time before we discover an entrance. The question then is: what will we find?

# CHAPTER 10

• • •

# THE BOOMERANG AND THE BIG ONE

THE COLD OF winter 1986 kept us from continual observation, even though the ships were flying, but by early spring we could get out of our cars long enough to enjoy the sightings.

In May 1986 I had a close range sighting of a new craft—the boomerang. In fact, it was a point-blank view. I had heard of the shape before—the *New York Times* had carried an article about the "Westchester Wing" in 1985—but I always thought people were mistaking the triangle by seeing it from a skewed perspective. That wasn't the case, I learned.

One evening I was alone on a back road, beside my car, taking pictures of lights in the sky. I'd been there only a few minutes when a craft came toward me from a field on my side of the road. Two other ships started closing in from a field on the other side.

The first craft stopped about thirty feet away. As I photographed it, the ship changed its lighting configuration completely. It slowly moved toward me. I was determined not to flee. It came directly to the car and stopped about eight feet or so above it. There was only a slight buzzing sound.

The craft had a central portion that was unlit and looked dark gray. That portion was geodesic ball-shaped, with a diameter of about eight feet, but its surface was made from angled planes rather than being rounded and smooth. Two wings extended from the central ball, giving the craft an overall width of perhaps twenty-five feet. The wings were thin and rectangular, tapering inward where they joined the ball. They were in sockets and movable. I saw them swivel in several directions. Under each wing were two doughnut-shaped red lights set in neon-type tubing so that they apparently would be visible only from a position almost directly below.

The ball section hung in the air over the passenger side of my car. One wing slowly fanned over me and the roof of the car. I started yelling, "What are you guys doing? Where's my ride? You owe me a conversation. Why are you doing things this way?"

But no answer came.

Then I started to get really nervous. I felt I'd been stupid to yell. After all, whoever was controlling the craft could easily see and hear me from their small cockpit, but I couldn't see or hear anything from them.

I examined details of the craft. It was so near I could have touched it. The wings seemed to be made of black metal and were not smooth. They had deep indentations and protrusions, as if machined parts had been pieced together, much the way our own spacecraft appear. The only clearly and easily seen portions of the wings were those directly around the red tube lights. As soon as my gaze moved from the lights, the metal couldn't easily be seen, even at my very close range of two to three feet.

I suddenly had an outrageous thought: I'd throw a pebble at the ship to see if it would "ping" off the metal. The pebbles were a few feet away at the roadside, but I didn't move. The craft started to back off. I snapped some more pictures. The other two ships across the street were still hanging there. Only after the boomerang moved away and ascended did the other ships begin to travel.

I was shaking, but this was a milestone for me. Not only

had I seen a new shape, it was also closer to me than any craft had been for quite a while—and I had stuck to my vow never to run away again. Walking to the edge of the road, I picked up a handful of small stones and said, "Next time, ship, I'm going to see if these ping off you."

Spring moved into summer. Since I was getting publicity now, my karate teacher, Rick Rohrman, asked to go along with me for a look at the ships. Other students in the school overheard him and asked also. The next thing I knew, half the dojo wanted to come. The next night a party of a dozen accompanied me.

The ships were flying all over with their lights on, but it was just distant viewing that time. We went back a second time—only ten were in the group now—and again the ships were flying lighted in the distance. Some of the people with me realized that airplanes can't stay stationary in the sky for the long periods of time that some of the lights were hovering there.

It was still too large a crowd for me to deal with, however, so I said "no" to many people. Rick began to come to Pine Bush regularly with his girlfriend, and sometimes without me. Several times they saw craft sitting on the ground and once, while they were standing in a field, one came toward them. At that point they got scared and left the field. But they are two more among the dozens of people who can testify to the presence of unidentified flying objects in the air above Pine Bush.

In September I decided to place an ad in the Middletown *Record*. The paper had run a Sunday feature story on me the previous year, so many people already knew about me and what I was undertaking there. I needed help from local residents. A classified ad seemed to be one way of getting in contact with them. So I ran this: "UFOs. Anyone seeing clear-cut craft contact me in confidence. Include date, place, time, brief account. I have taken more than three hundred photos of these craft. Write: UFOs, Box 12, New Milford, NJ 07646."

I received dozens of letters. One came from Robert Toto of Montgomery, the town just east of Pine Bush. Bob was a field representative for MUFON—the Mutual UFO Network, a well-respected national investigative organization based in Seguin, Texas. He had been trained as a behavioral psychologist and was a part-time hypnotherapist. I called him and we agreed to meet at his home. His wife, Joan, was skeptical about the whole situation and declined to go to the fields with us. But Nicole, his young daughter, sometimes accompanied us and was present for one of our most spectacular sightings.

Bob and I saw many craft on many occasions, but he wanted to keep his role inconspicuous so as not to draw a crowd. We were out in the fields several times a week and had many incredible sightings in which we both took many photographs. When Bob got a video camera, his recordings proved extremely interesting. He did not officially involve MUFON or submit reports to headquarters.

Bob taught an adult education class in parapsychology and began bringing people from the class into the fields with us. He had decided that more people should see the phenomena so we would all be better off. Some of them also had excellent sightings.

In March, 1990, Bob passed away suddenly. The void he left is felt every time we go to Pine Bush and realize his car won't be parked at the side of the road when we get there.

In mid-November I spoke on UFOs and showed some of my photos at a conference in New Haven, Connecticut, sponsored by Donna Sommers, publisher of *Balance* magazine, and psychic-artist Rev. Ed Morét. Both Donna and Ed had accompanied me to Pine Bush one night a few months earlier, where we saw a spectacular UFO. Ed had tape recorded his awed reaction upon seeing it. He played it by way of introducing me to help the audience share the reality of what we'd seen, and people seemed to be amazed.

Another of the speakers was John White, an author and

investigator of paranormal phenomena. We met shortly after the conference began and quickly struck up a friendship.
John felt I had something important to say about the UFO
phenomenon, and he invited me to present my work the
following year at a conference he produces annually, "The
UFO Experience." After the New Haven conference, John
joined me in Pine Bush on half a dozen occasions, sometimes bringing other interested people. His statement is
given in Appendix 1.

The year 1986 ended with a spectacular sighting when I
was all alone. I was standing beside my car as usual on a
dirt road I frequently visit, watching the ships fly up and
down the tree line in front of where they land. The tree line
was formed by dense forest through which streams meandered. One stream was about ten feet wide and a yard deep
in spots. I didn't want to risk going through in the daytime,
let alone at night. To get to the fields on the other side of
the trees, I would have to drive around the block—that's a
country block, maybe half a mile wide—and enter from the
other side. By that time, the ships would have taken off. I
know; I'd tried it before.

So I remained on the roadside, observing the tree line,
when suddenly an absolutely monstrous-sized craft lifted
above the trees and came toward me from the field on the
other side. It was enormous. It seemed as wide as the field
itself. As it moved toward me, it began ascending. There
was no noise from it but the ground started to shake, and
as it almost reached me, I heard a horrible sound like a
grinding motor. The ground continued to shake. I got scared
but had sufficient presence of mind to keep my tape recorder running and my camera clicking away. I couldn't
see the exact shape of the craft, but its size made the largest
of the other craft I'd seen—those with a perimeter of three
hundred feet or so—look like mosquitoes. I could hardly
believe it had been sitting in someone's farm field.

I began to tell my acquaintances about it and call it "the
Big One" and "the Jumbo." I also wanted to see it again,

at least once more. January 1987 was too cold to go to the fields, but one February night Bob Toto and I went out to view the sky. We'd just stopped the car next to a farm field when, no more than a minute later, the Big One lifted off behind the tree line and came toward us. All we could say at first was, "Oh, my God! Oh, my God!"

There was no rumbling of the ground as the tremendous ship flew past us. We couldn't even hear it until it moved overhead. But it was beautiful and it made our night. Bob was ecstatic. This event was to mark another change in the ships' sizes and behavior.

In February, 1987 we had some amazing sightings of the Big One coming over the trees toward us. I made several tape recordings of its sound. One night, however, it passed by silently, right overhead without any noise at all. The ships, regardless of their size, are capable of silent propulsion. Yet, on occasion they rumbled or made awful metallic noises. Why they do so is anyone's guess. A lack of noise is contrary to everything we are used to about machine propulsion. Jets and propeller-driven planes roar. Even whisper jets can be so loud that you can't hear a person talk, yet there in the Pine Bush area, ships were flying with no noise. It was like watching a movie without the speaker on. Surreal, perhaps, but not unreal. I believe the silence of the ships contributes to the widespread notion that UFOs are harmless and here for human benefit. When no noise is involved, a situation seems less threatening.

In early March, I took a spectacular photograph of a large craft that was apparently near us in a field, although we didn't—or couldn't—see it. The twenty or so assorted horizontal lights in various shapes and colors had shown up, in part, on many other photos over the years. But in this instance I had the full craft—taken with flash to light up the foreground and foliage—looking like it was five feet above ground and about thirty feet away, even though it still didn't show up on film.

That made me angry. It's happened many times, and I've

1. POD MARK. Pine Bush, N.Y. Taken July, 1985, of a depression two feet by three feet in the ground that we saw being made on March 30 or 31, 1985.

2. POD MARK. Pine Bush, N.Y. This two feet by three feet patch was in the cemetery for a couple of years with nothing growing in it, from about 1985 to 1987. I made the mistake of telling the cemetery managers about it and they dug up the plot and sodded it.

3. LARGE MULTI-COLORED TESLA ON GROUND. Pine Bush, N.Y. September 9, 1986. I drove down the street, saw lights over the trees, got out and took a picture, got back in my car, and drove down to our usual spot. It's incredible that this huge thing is sitting invisible to our eyes, close to the road, and I happened to stop at its exact location to take the photo.

4. TESLA GLOBES WITH "PLANE." Pine Bush, N.Y. August 10, 1988. We watched a light moving across the field not knowing what it was. It suddenly turned and came directly at us. With its conventional lighting, we weren't even sure what it was. Everyone was shocked to see the Teslas around the object in the photo.

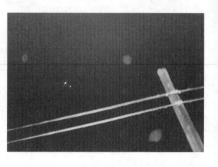

5. BEAM OF LIGHT. Pine Bush, N.Y. October, 1987. In 1987 we began getting photos of poles of light along some of the roads where sightings were the heaviest. We must have seen lights over the field and snapped the picture. An electronics expert looked at the pictures and thought they might be beacons coming up from the ground.

6. ROW OF LIGHTS. Pine Bush, N.Y. April, 1987. About ten people watched a red light go down in the woods and decided we should go there. Coming back out of the woods into the field, I decided to take a picture of the field. We were astonished when we saw the row of lights in the photos.

7. LARGE TESLA FIELD. Pine Bush, N.Y. June 12, 1988. We watched a craft go down and ran into the field. Something else came toward us in this next field and two of us took photos. The other camera had a zoom lens, so in addition to my photo here, we got a close-up of this Tesla.

8. WANAQUE RESERVOIR, N.J. February, 1981. This is a five minute time exposure of a craft that hovered and rotated over the reservoir for twenty minutes. This chunk of light is higher in the sky than the craft was visually. The craft didn't register on film—only these emissions invisible to our eyes.

9. TESLA AND TELEPHONE POLE. Pine Bush, N.Y. July, 1987. Many lights were flying and it wasn't even dark. We're not sure if the Tesla is in front of the pole, or behind it.

10. GROUP OF LIGHTS. Pine Bush, N.Y. January, 1985. We saw a flashing strobe in the cemetery area and I snapped the picture. The perspective of the lights show bottom and sides of the craft.

11. SCATTERED TESLAS. Pine Bush, N.Y. June 14, 1988. When there are lots of lights flying, there seems to be much more going on than we can see, as on this night.

12. BRIGHT LIGHT WITH ANGLED RAYS AND SMALL GLOBE ON GROUND. Montgomery, N.Y. July, 1986. Series of two. We were in a different area of fields when the craft came head-on toward us. The small globe on the ground crops up once in a while when photographing ships. I'm not sure if it's a Tesla globe, another craft on the ground, or their machinery.

13. FORMATION OF OBJECTS. Bergen County, N.J. October, 1981. Five minute time exposure at 10:00 PM (star trails can be seen). We watched more than twenty objects circling the sky for hours. I took a roll of film and this was the only picture to register anything.

14. LARGE TESLA GLOBE. Pine Bush, N.Y. July, 1989. We were watching lights from the road when I snapped this shot.

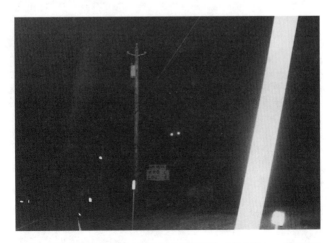

15. TWO PAIRS OF DUAL LIGHTS. Middletown, N.Y. February 21, 1990. Series of eight. I watched one large object with unusual brilliant white lights come toward me. I never saw the second set of dim reddish lights above it.

16. TRIANGLE CRAFT. Pine Bush, N.Y. July, 1980. What we saw was a clear-cut metallic triangle craft. The film registered what our eyes didn't see: shortwave radiation discharges coming off the craft out of vents.

17. TRIANGLE CRAFT WITH EMANATIONS. Pine Bush, N.Y. July, 1980. When this triangle craft was about thirty feet above me, it turned to me and stopped in midair. What we saw of the craft were large windows and a bowed plus-sign lighting panel. For this discharge to cover the craft this thoroughly, it would have to come out of vents around the windows, or the lighting system itself, be giving off the discharge around the whole ship, which would explain why we couldn't photograph what we saw.

18. TWO ALIENS AT REAR OF TRIANGLE CRAFT. Pine Bush, N.Y. July, 1980. We saw the craft on the ground flashing many lights. More than a year passed before I enlarged this set of pictures and realized what I really had in the photographs.

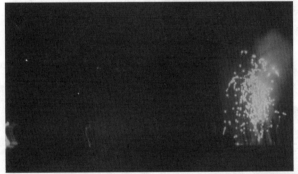

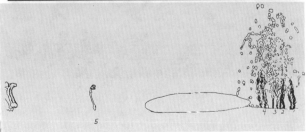

19. FIVE ALIENS AT TRIANGLE CRAFT ON GROUND. Pine Bush, N.Y. July, 1980. Four stand in the spray at right and one in the center frame. This photo was taken four frames and a couple of minutes after the "Two Aliens" photograph. We assumed someone was at the craft on the ground but we didn't see anyone.

always felt frustrated and mad. The ships were still playing games with me. They wanted me and those with me to know they were there, but on their terms. Too many photos had been blanked out in some of the spectacular close sightings. It was as if a tradeoff were being made. "You want to see us up close? Then no photographs. You want photos? See if you can find us."

Surprisingly, almost all of my photos of these unseen craft are perfectly centered in the frame. Someone was guiding me. I knew because I could "feel" them.

These feelings were to intensify in importance in 1988—as I describe in chapter 11—when several people accompanying me to Pine Bush complained about different bodily sensations when around the ships, both in previous encounters at other locations and in Pine Bush.

I was always distinctly aware of my own sensations because I had experienced the aliens' energy—or vibes—as early as 1980, and used it to home in on where the ships were. But I never talked about the actual sensations; I would simply say I could "feel" the ships. I never really explained what I was feeling until several people in succession started talking about their own "feelings."

We now use these sensations as a working tool to guide us. We've found that different parts of the body seem to feel the variations of the energy fields used by the aliens. A blind person, properly trained to recognize these sensations, would be able to know an alien's presence as clearly as a sighted person.

Half the time I didn't even think about what I was doing; I simply focused and shot at the open sky. It never ceased to amaze me to find spectacular images on my commercially processed film—images that were clear-cut lights from a craft, even though, out in the field, my colleagues and I couldn't see them because our eyes are so limited in perceptual range.

As the spring went on and the weather got nicer, people asked to go to Pine Bush with me. I was continually looking for people who might enhance the situation by encouraging the ships to allow closer encounters. After all, who wants to just see lights when you have a chance to see a craft totally?

One April night in 1987, half a dozen of us were standing on a dirt road beside a field I often visited when we saw a ship rise and descend behind the tree line about a quarter of a mile away. Four of us walked through the field to see what we could up close. It was a bright evening with a full moon, and after walking about one hundred feet or so into the woods, we realized how difficult it would be to go on. A large stream meandered through the area, which was otherwise rather boggy. We ran into some barbed wire also. As the going got tougher and the terrain swampier, we decided to go back. Peering as far as we could through the trees, we could see nothing.

As we came out of the woods, I aimed my camera into the field and took a picture. I was very familiar with this field, having spent much time looking into it and photographing it from the road, so I thought I would shoot it from a new angle. When I got the film back from Fotomat, the multilighted craft I had photographed the month before in that field was again in the photo with slightly different lights on. The craft had lights in various shapes and colors, yet none of us had seen it. I must have "felt" it, though, because as usual, it was dead-center in my frame, and only a few feet off the ground.

John White had been one of the party. When he looked at the photos a few weeks later, he was perplexed. He had trekked across the field into the woods. How could we have missed it, he wondered, when the evening was so bright. I hated the fact that the ships were passing close to us but we couldn't see them.

By May, the ships were back in full swing and we were about to have a summer of fascinating sightings once again.

# CHAPTER 11

* * *

# MEDIA EXPOSURE AND
# THE BIRTH OF CONTACTEE

In 1987, THE media began to take more notice of my research. Occasional articles had appeared in local newspapers and magazines—*Omni, Photomethods*, even the *National Examiner*—plus the *PM Magazine* segment, but a letter I wrote to the publisher of the *New York Times* initiated a chain of events that raised my public visibility quite a bit. I wrote in August to complain that the *Times* wasn't covering a big event—the Pine Bush story. On September 2, 1987, Arthur Ochs Sulzberger, the publisher, replied:

> Dear Ms. Crystall:
> We have a great many distinguished science writers working for the *New York Times* and, to the best of my knowledge, none of them believe in UFOs and, I might add, neither do I. So I am afraid we are going to continue the current policy of skepticism until there are some harder facts.
>
> Sincerely,
> Arthur Ochs Sulzberger

I was irritated by Sulzberger's attitude because it seemed to go beyond skepticism into cynicism, including a refusal even to look into the story. To his credit, however, he wasn't closed to the possibility of gathering more facts. He passed my letter to a reporter/columnist, Michael Winerip. Several weeks later Michael contacted me about going to Pine Bush. I invited him to join me the following Saturday night. I'd already planned to meet with John White, who in turn wanted me to meet two of his friends, a well-known abductee, Marianne Shenefield, and her husband, Dan, who live in Agawam, Massachusetts. John had asked Marianne and me to speak at his November conference, "The UFO Experience," in North Haven, Connecticut. The conference has since become a successful annual event, but this one was the first and its success was uncertain. It was to get needed publicity, via the column.

Michael and I met in New Jersey, drove to Pine Bush, and met with John, Marianne, and Dan. Over supper we became acquainted and discussed various aspects of the UFO situation. Michael was properly cautious in listening to my story, asking questions of us all, cross-checking with other data he had, and generally probing to find out what was going on—hoax, shared delusion, aliens from space, or what.

After our meal we drove to Searsville Road, Michael and I in his car; Dan and Marianne in John's. It was not a good night. Overcast skies and heavy rain made a sighting unlikely. It seems the ships don't like to fly under certain meteorological conditions, especially rain. Since the alleged crash of a UFO near Roswell, New Mexico, in 1947 during a thunderstorm, it may be that the aliens have good reason to avoid those conditions. That's only speculation, but we saw nothing that night. I was disappointed, but Michael had a column to write, and he had sufficient material to do so. Several weeks later he published it. One sentence in the full-page column mentioned that John was "running a UFO conference at the Ramada Inn in North Haven" but nothing else. The motel switchboard was inundated with calls.

Michael wrote:

Ms. Crystall and her UFO associates, who all hold down jobs during the day, know some people think this is crazy. "I don't care," she says. "If a friend isn't interested, I don't impose my views." However, she does feel a duty to complain to newspapers if their UFO coverage is weak. Her letters are well written. . . .

She estimates she has seen 1,000 UFO's. "It's ridiculous," she says, "so many." There are a couple of airports near here, but Ms. Crystall says it's easy to recognize a UFO: "It comes from looking at so many. I can feel them. Even if something looks like an airplane, I'll say, 'wait a minute, that's a ship.' It might have yellow lights—planes don't have yellow lights. . . ."

Later, four of them sat in their cars in the rain for more than an hour . . . but there was nothing. "When you see one, it's fantastic," Ms. Crystall said. "Makes up for all the wasted nights." She was home early, by 11.

The Stewart Airport fire chief, Arnold Messer, has heard the UFO tales. "There's a group of pilots from the airport near here at Stormville who like to pretend to be UFOs" he said. "They fly in formation for just that reason." He said they put different color lights on their planes to fake people out. "We see them," he said, "we just say, 'the boys at Stormville are at it again.' "

The *Times* is read not just nationally, but internationally, as well, so the result of Michael's column was an immediate rush of phone calls to me from people all over the planet. Most of the calls were from the U.S., of course, but I received calls from Canada, Great Britain, and Australia. Most came from people who wanted more information or who wanted to share their experiences. Many were from the media, however, primarily talk radio programs wanting to book me for a conversation with their listeners, and reporters who wanted to interview me for their newspapers.

One was from the *Geraldo Rivera Show*, which originates in New York City. The show was taped in late October and aired on November 2, 1987. When I received the call, it was exciting to think of the opportunity for a soapbox to tell my story nationally, but what actually happened was disappointing. The producer originally intended to have me on stage with Budd Hopkins, Bruce Maccabee, and the other guests. As it turned out, I was seated in the audience and my appearance was limited to about three minutes in which to explain some of my photos.

I also appeared on *People Are Talking* from WWOR in Secaucus, New Jersey. I told my story and showed some photos in the usual manner. In the audience that morning was David De Lia, a disc jockey who was working at WJLK, a Top 40 radio station in Asbury Park, New Jersey. Some weeks later Dave contacted me to go to Pine Bush, and that was the beginning of a very wonderful relationship, both professional and personal. Dave had seen UFOs on several occasions in New York and New Jersey. He began going to Pine Bush with me and others becoming a staunch colleague.

Another media contact resulting from the *Times* column came from the Copley Radio Network, a news service for radio station subscribers. In early November, Copley profiled me in *Wireless Flash*, its summary sheet of interesting and available personalities. The story went to about one thousand radio stations around the United States, Canada, Australia, and New Zealand.

The result was a veritable deluge of invitations to speak. Over the next few months I talked on dozens of shows throughout North America, Europe, and Australia. The experience was both heady and wearying. I spoke for the same reason I've written this book: to share this important message. But as any author or media personality can testify, high visibility has its price, including exhaustion and loss of privacy.

About this time I found that many people were interested

enough in research and support on a continuing basis that I began to wonder what I might do to tap this vein. Reflecting on the situation, the idea of a formal organization began to grow and I decided to create the first organization for research into the UFO phenomenon by direct observation.

Thus, in the spring of 1988, Contactee was born. Contactee is an organization primarily for people who have had close encounters of the second, third, fourth, and fifth kinds. However, anyone can join. I publish a quarterly newsletter, *Contactee*, and have an advisory board. Our goal is to educate the public about what is occurring worldwide by making current information available about where UFOs are being sighted and what observers experience. Any funds go for field research, equipment, and publication costs for the newsletter. Members are invited to tell their observations and conclusions through the newsletter, so Contactee does not represent anyone's particular viewpoint, even my own. If you'd like to join or learn more about it, my address is given at the end of the book.

Our activities at Pine Bush continued to get national attention. In October an Associated Press reporter, David Bauder, learned of me and asked to be taken along. I agreed. The night we went was cloudy and, as Bauder later quoted me as saying, "It was a crummy night." I'd arranged for Peter Gersten and Bauder to meet myself and Dave De Lia in Pine Bush. Peter is an attorney and a member of CAUS—Citizens Against UFO Secrecy—which is dedicated to breaking through the government cover-up of the truth about the phenomenon. Peter, on behalf of CAUS, sued the United States government for access to classified material that CAUS had learned about. The case went all the way to the Supreme Court, where CAUS lost on grounds of national security. The details of this landmark event in ufology appear in *Clear Intent* (recently retitled *The UFO Cover-up*) by Lawrence Fawcett and Barry Greenwood, both CAUS members. *Clear Intent* is an important book for documenting the government cover-up.

When we got to Pine Bush, Peter and Bauder were waiting by his Porsche with a license plate reading "UFOSREAL." Half a dozen other people were there beside their cars. Peter greeted us humorously with, "You missed it, Ellen. The mother ship was here. There used to be several more of us waiting."

As it turned out, waiting was just about all that happened that night. It grew late and cold, and the evening ended in disappointment. But Bauder had come for a story, so he told it like it happened and sent it over the wires. Consequently, people all over the U.S. and Canada soon read about "Hot Spot for UFO Fans," as the *Los Angeles Times* headline for the article read on November 20, 1988. "N.Y.'s Hudson Valley Draws the Hopeful Faithful Each Night," it proclaimed in a subheading as if I were leading a cult. Nothing could be further from the truth than that thought, though; I want *coworkers* in this tremendously important research. We need more resources—equipment and money—and dedicated but tough-minded people who'll do the hard field work and rigorous analysis of the data. And if the truth turns out to be what I suspect about these aliens, "faithful" would be the worst possible attitude to take toward them. The general public seems to have two principal images about UFO occupants: space brothers and space invaders. All that I've experienced so far leads me toward the second possibility.

# CHAPTER 12

• • •

# ALIEN VIBES

THROUGHOUT 1988 I gained a more precise understanding of the physiological feelings apparently caused by ships or their energy fields. When I first met Dave De Lia, he said that whenever ships were present, whether he was standing around or driving on a highway, with no warning and even without a visual sighting, his hair would stand on end and he would shiver. I understood but didn't tell him specifically what I experienced; I only said I, too, could feel the aliens' vibes.

In March I met a lawyer at a UFO conference on Long Island who spoke with me to get some insight about unusual experiences he and his family were having at their farm, in Dutchess County, New York. I was indeed interested when I heard his account because it sounded like a case of multiple abductions. I decided to inspect the farm. I told Dave about it and he offered to go along.

On a Saturday night in June 1988, we drove there. As we arrived in the area, Dave started to shiver as he does when ships are nearby. We saw a light over the fields to our left, but it veered away and we lost it. Then we were at the farm.

Their home was a modern, glass-faced house at the right front corner of a two-acre plot. A small barn and paddock were behind and to the left. The rest of the property was field and forest. No horses were in the paddock, though. The lawyer had gotten rid of them because they were so restless all night, apparently due to the presence of ships.

We climbed through the fence toward the back field, but Dave started to shiver and got upset, saying, "There's something here. . . ." We went back to the fence, climbed through, and went toward the house. There definitely was a different "feel" between the house area and the field. We looked around but didn't see any air activity.

Dark clouds were rolling in, and it looked like rain. We walked around the field again, then returned to the car. Dave aimed his 35mm automatic camera upward and took a photo. He also aimed into the field and took a flash photo. Then we left.

Several weeks later we were shocked to see prints of what Dave had shot. Right above our heads was a clear blue Tesla globe, just like the ones in Pine Bush. This was Dave's first photo. The second photo, taken of the field, was even more surprising. It looked as if whitish curtains or veils of translucent fabric covered the immediate vicinity. Fuller descriptions can be seen in chapter 16.

Another incident with alien energy occurred one evening the following November as Dave and I were leaving the radio station where he worked. I could feel the ships around. I didn't say anything to Dave, but no sooner had we gotten into his car and driven for no more than two minutes when something unseen hit us without warning. It felt like a beam of energy. I gasped as it took my breath away. I would have been knocked down if I hadn't been sitting in the car. At the same time as I gasped, Dave said, "Oh, my God. . . ."

I said, "I got it, too."

We looked up and saw a flashing light fly a short distance and then dim out. I thought the light was too high for what we felt and that something must be closer.

Dave was excited, saying, "You got it, too? Then I'm

not imagining things. The creepy vibes I get when the ships are around are real.''

I asked, ''That's how strong the vibes are that you get when you're in Pine Bush?''

He said yes, they always were. He had been complaining about them for the six months he'd been going to Pine Bush. He had experienced the same thing during his earlier sightings before contacting me.

''No wonder you're always shivering and upset when you feel them, if they're that strong.''

My colleagues and I had other extraordinary experiences with ''alien energy,'' not always at Pine Bush. In 1986, several friends and I were sitting around the living room at the home of my girl friend Eleanor. A movement I glimpsed out of the corner of my eye made me turn my head. I saw a reddish-brown dustlike cloud about three feet across coming through her living room toward me. The cloud had jagged edges. As the cloud moved past me, one of the edges touched me. My body spasmed in a way I'd already come to recognize as indicative of alien energy.

The cloud then touched Jimmy, one of the people in the room. It passed through his body shoulder to shoulder and vanished. The moment it touched him, his eyes rolled upward into his head and he fell back, exclaiming, ''Oh, my God, you are going to have the most incredible abduction experience. . . .'' He then described it in detail, but couldn't say when it would happen because he didn't know.

Since no one else in the room saw or felt the cloud, they were all surprised by our outbursts. Jimmy couldn't believe the alien feeling and kept asking about it. He finally had to leave, stumbling out of the apartment, almost incoherent. To date, his prediction has not come true, but I still consider it a possibility.

Another person in the Pine Bush group who feels alien energy is a registered nurse, Helen. She gets the same sensations as Dave, and when she first described them, they sounded rather frightening to us. More than once she scared us into our cars and out of the immediate area.

Although I had always felt physical sensations, until Helen came along, I really didn't know how to explain to people what I was feeling or even why. I knew that some people who were used to chasing after ships through the fields would get sensations that they interpreted as fear or just as ''the creeps'' and would want to leave. On several occasions we parked at the Jewish cemetery, got out of the car, and got horrendous vibes. I felt them in my solar plexus—painfully to the point where I'd have to leave the area. I wondered whether these feelings were due to some sort of alien security system that disturbs human physiology to the point of discomfort to drive away unwanted visitors. If so, it works beautifully. My sensitive colleagues and I have at times gone away distraught, knowing something was there but unable to pinpoint what and where.

One evening we went to the cemetery, and I felt something as soon as we arrived. I pushed on the entrance gates and felt something physically holding them back. I told the people with me that there definitely was something more than just buried people in there. I put my camera through the gate and took a flash photo. So did the others.

When film came back from processing, I had a photo of three large translucent blue-green ''mounds of energy'' over the cemetery. No one else got any images. The gravestones can be seen through the blue-green areas because, as usual, the flash lit up the foreground.

The aliens have specific vibes, distinctly different from human vibes, which is another reason they can't casually walk among us. There is also a distinct difference between the vibes their machinery gives off and their vibes as beings.

I had a very disturbing experience in June 1987 in Brewster, New York, where I was a speaker at a conference on the Hudson Valley UFO sightings. I was waiting in the rear of the auditorium to be introduced. As a member of the audience finished describing his experience, I walked up the aisle to wait to be introduced.

Large spotlights were lighting the stage area. As I was introduced and approached the stage, I stepped into the lighted area. A blast of alien energy hit me like a hard slap on the back.

I lurched forward and turned around to see what had done it, only to be blinded by the spotlights. No one had visibly touched me. The "hit" had come from where I had been standing in the back of the auditorium—where the only doors to the outside were. Something had cleverly entered the room and, as I stepped into the lights, blasted me, knowing I would be blinded by the spotlights and that I couldn't do anything about it.

I was very shaken and asked for a brief break so I could set up my slides. As I worked with the projector, I continually looked at the back doors, where "something" was. It was dark and crowded back there; I couldn't distinguish the source of the attack, nor could I walk back to look around because time was pressing.

When I finished my slide presentation and prepared for questions from the audience, I suddenly realized that if someone were to ask a question about the aliens, I could indicate that something alien was in the auditorium. But no one asked such a question, which only added to my upset feelings.

When I finished, it was time for the supper break, so I hurried to some of my friends to tell them what had happened. They became upset, too, and looked around for whatever might be there, but it was long gone, probably right after my slide presentation was over and the auditorium lights went on.

# CHAPTER 13

• • •

# WHERE HAVE ALL THE SAUCERS GONE? THE MANY SHAPES OF CRAFT

WHEN THE MODERN era of UFO sightings began shortly after World War II, the term for what I call the ships was "flying saucers." It was coined by a journalist to denote what Kenneth Arnold, a civilian pilot, saw in June 1947—nine objects moving through the sky at high speed near Mt. Ranier, Washington, with a motion like a rock being skipped across the surface of a pond. Arnold told a reporter the objects looked like two saucers inverted on one another. And because they were airborne, they became "flying" saucers.

The term quickly caught on, even though within a few years it became obvious that not all the unusual aerial objects being seen were saucer-shaped. Some were cigar-shaped. By the 1960s, a wide variety of shapes and sizes had been seen. They were assorted, but certain basic types could be discerned, with variations on them. Clearly, "saucer" was not a comprehensive term. Thus, "unidentified flying object" gained general usage among researchers, gradually displacing the older term.

Some books emphasizing the saucerlike shape were written by authors who weren't interested in first-hand research and personal observation. These authors didn't—and still don't—understand why there are different shapes. They generated wild theories that are better classified as science fiction. For example, one writer held that the different shapes were used by different races of aliens visiting us. Several other writers maintained that UFOs had the ability to change shape and to dematerialize. These statements have been widely proclaimed by authors and their readers, but the only result has been to mislead the public into a false perspective about UFOs—a perspective that still has not changed.

By the late 1970s, almost no saucerlike shapes were reported, yet the media and authors of many books on UFOs never looked at the newer sightings that described triangular-shaped craft. People who had seen saucer-shaped UFOs in the 1960s or early 1970s were sighting angular UFOs and were confused by what they now saw.

When I was in California in 1971, I saw the classically formed flying saucers. But my closest encounter—which I described in chapter 1—was with an angular craft. It wasn't until 1980 in Pine Bush that I saw an entire craft at point-blank range and realized it was the same angular shape as the craft I had seen in California.

At the onset of our Pine Bush sightings, we saw only craft that I refer to as "triangles." Soon afterward, we had a clear sighting of a rectangular or boxcar-shaped craft. The triangle had a perimeter of about two hundred feet; the rectangle was about three hundred feet. We also saw other UFOs that were shaped differently from these.

For example, in the summer of 1986, several of us watched a very large craft that looked to me like a turtle's body flying overhead. Someone called it "walnut-shaped" and I thought that description was better. This craft seemed to be about five hundred feet around. At times it made a horrendous noise; at other times it made no noise at all.

In late 1986 we began to see ships with a perimeter greater than five hundred feet, taking off from farm fields. These craft appeared to be solid, diamond-shaped, and almost the color of rusty metal. I also saw, as mentioned earlier, a small boomerang-shaped craft which was about twenty-five feet from tip to tip. Many people have reported larger boomerangs—I've not seen them—which appear to be roughly the same size as what I call triangles. At first I thought people were simply making a mistake and were actually seeing triangles from a different perspective, but now that doesn't seem to be the case. Boomerangs come in small and large varieties.

Here is a summary of the types of craft I've observed around Pine Bush:

> *Triangle*—most are about sixty feet on each side, two hundred feet in perimeter. A larger one is about four hundred feet in perimeter.
>
> *Diamond shape*—about four hundred feet in perimeter.
>
> *Rectangle*—about three hundred feet in perimeter.
>
> *Boomerang*—the small one is about twenty-five feet from tip to tip. The large one appears to be about two hundred feet in perimeter.
>
> *Walnut* or *turtle shape*—about four hundred feet or more in perimeter.
>
> *Manta ray shape*—about four hundred feet in perimeter.
>
> *Jumbo* or *Big One*—about five hundred feet in perimeter; has two "noses" and "wings."
>
> *Small airplane*—about twenty-five feet wingtip to wingtip; has a black body, silver wings, no wheels or apparent engines.

All of these craft operate silently, although on occasion they make a wide assortment of noises. Sometimes their sound gets louder *after* they have passed over us, and it is a deliberate, sudden change in volume, not a gradual increase.

The different craft seem to have various purposes. Classically-shaped flying saucers are used for abductions. Triangles are scout-type ships. Rectangles have been seen in conjunction with animal mutilations. Extremely large craft, particularly those with rows of red lights surrounding a clearly visible metallic-looking seam implying a loading platform, would be for carrying cargo to and from our planet. (I was stunned when I got a clear view of this craft one night. It was a clear indication that supplies were being brought in and that there was indeed an installation at which to unload them.)

The craft also appear to use different types of power or several different types of power each.

A few weeks after I began going to Pine Bush in 1980, I saw what seemed like small planes mixed in with the ships. My initial impression was that some local pilots had gotten wise to the ships and were going after them, which seemed quite dangerous. Their actions seemed illogical too until I later observed that the planes seemed to have the alien's technology. Moreover, they didn't seem to be making any noise. On one occasion in 1980, when we watched a small plane fly at treetop level and suddenly reverse its direction without turning around, we knew something was different than what it appeared to be. I asked Bruce and Wendy why there were planes among the ships. They answered that the aliens had their own planes. I thought their statement was crazy, but an incident in 1984 changed my mind and left me astonished by the implications.

On that occasion, Cathy and I were leaving Pine Bush at night. As we came to the crest of a hill next to some fields, two flashing lights raced toward us at treetop height. I stopped the car. The two lights just hung there, flashing. It looked almost as if the aliens were deciding what kind of stunt to pull on us.

I continued driving south, and as we reached Route 17 in New Jersey, one of the lights followed us, paralleling the highway and matching the speed of my car. As I slowed to take the Oradell exit, the craft halted in the sky with a skidding motion, almost like a vehicle in a cartoon would stop. Then it descended much lower, moving toward the car even though we were still driving.

We turned onto the main town road. The ship dropped behind some houses but continued paralleling us. It turned on many of its lights. Cathy readied her camera while I looked for a spot to pull over because other cars were on the road and too many houses obstructed our view.

About a block farther on, I started to pull off the road. The ship suddenly turned on many lights and headed toward the roof of the house next to us, skimmed over the top of it and headed directly toward us! I jammed on the brakes, stopped in the middle of the road, and we both jumped out, leaving the doors wide open. Cathy and I clicked off four photos of what we clearly saw was a small airplane, about twenty feet across from wingtip to wingtip, with a black body and silver wings. No propellors or engines of any type were visible, and it was virtually noiseless.

The "airplane" lifted one wing to pass over a small tree next to us. (We later measured the tree. It was about fifteen feet high, so the craft was barely fifteen feet above the ground.) The black metal of the fuselage was startling to look at. The metallic surface was quite smooth, although we could still see grooves and seams in the metal. The silver wings were also fairly smooth. (Many of the larger ships I've seen have many panels, deep grooves and contours, showing there is no wasted space on an alien craft.)

At the plane's closest point to us—about ten feet away— we could barely hear a buzzing sound. The craft flew past us at about five miles per hour, continued past the nearest house, then stopped in midair.

Now, it was one o'clock in the morning on a Saturday— Sunday morning, actually—and a few cars were on the road, passing by. My car was stopped in the middle of the road with its doors wide open. We—two women—were standing on the front lawn of a home, with cameras raised to our eyes, yet no one stopped to ask what was going on.

I thought that was probably more weird than seeing the ship/plane.

The craft turned around but remained about thirty feet from us, in full view. I wanted to see it better, without traffic around. We drove to a small park about half a mile down the road, but the craft did not follow us.

The next day I returned to the site to ask the people in the house the craft had flown over if they had been watching television at the time. When craft are near homes, they cause static and snow on television sets. But the man in the house told me he and his wife had been out at that hour and the children had been asleep.

I was left with some disconcerting thoughts. What if the aliens had built their own airplanes or had made their craft resemble ours? UFOs are only identified by their unearthly shapes and behavior. No one would look twice at an airplane coming through the sky—unless it stopped in midair or did something of which our technology is incapable, precisely as I had seen. The aliens had complete freedom of the skies if they disguised their craft as conventional aircraft and no one suspected what was flying by.

This smelled of invasion—in every sense of the word. It was bad enough that aliens were running around the planet, abducting people and disrupting their lives. If there was any ethical code of noninterference, it had been broken thousands of times over the years, through close encounters with humans. But to plan the entire charade so as to also give themselves unimpeded use of our airways was incredible. Something devious was going on. The aliens were not on the level about anything; they looked really untrustworthy and made me suspicious.

Why, I asked myself. What was so important that they would come to this planet unannounced, work undercover on the ground, and need freedom of the sky—all undetected except when they chose to reveal themselves? If they were so superior, why didn't they simply disclose themselves and take what they wanted? Humanity couldn't have stopped them. They, in turn, could have given us some kind of knowledge, which would surely be advanced beyond ours, and we would have been satisfied.

The more I thought about it, the more questions I had. The implications were profoundly disturbing. By human standards, you don't sneak in your neighbor's yard unless you're doing something he or she wouldn't approve of. If you have nothing to hide, if you're not up to some devious act, you just knock on your neighbor's front door and ask if you can look around.

The aliens must have known how fascinating they were to us, especially to scientists and ufologists who have spent their lives seeking extraterrestrial contact or evidence of it. The aliens must also have known how confusing they were to us, especially in close encounters.

They had planned everything so perfectly. When my colleagues and I ran through the fields after them, they had many means of distracting us or giving us the thrill of a close encounter, knowing we would be satisfied for the moment. And we reacted exactly as they wanted. Only once in a while could I trick them by doing something differently at the last minute. They were unprepared when I did the unexpected; they were not omniscient and had a limited range of control over me.

What could they have been doing, I asked myself. I was sure they were drilling and had machinery operating. Dale and Mark told me the aliens were mining beryllium, zirconium, and titanium.

I pursued this clue via library research. Amazingly, I learned that the three metals were not only rare but were found only in some small Asian countries and—I nearly flipped out at this fact—in Orange County, New York, exactly where I was pursuing the ships. It is interesting to note that these metals are used in nuclear reactor plants.

I learned another startling fact about the location: the Wallkill River, which runs through most of the area, is one of only several rivers in the continental United States to run north instead of south. The water table is abnormally high in the Pine Bush area. Some ufologists have theorized that UFOs have some technological connection with water. I never believed that the connection was real; otherwise, UFOs would land in lakes and ponds rather than farm fields. What UFOs would want with the Wallkill River is unclear to me. Nevertheless, the information about the river made me uncomfortable.

As with my photographs, it seemed as if facts and re-curring patterns were deliberately kept out of the UFO picture by sabotage or disinformation.

And where, I wondered, do humans fit into the picture? Everything seems so one-sided in the aliens' direction. Are they doing something to help us or hinder us—or harm us? Or is it totally irrelevant to human life? In short, what is the human factor?

# CHAPTER 14

### • • •

# THE HUMAN FACTOR

IF I RELIED on only my own experiences with the aliens
and their ships, I would say that we humans are irrelevant
to their purpose and thus they feel we don't have to know
anything about them. But, like all serious researchers, I do
not operate in a vacuum. I try to stay abreast of develop-
ments in this field by reading the professional publications,
by attending conferences, and by interacting with other investigators through correspondence, telephone calls, and
personal meetings.

Nor do I claim to have a monopoly on truth and to be
offering *the* answer to the UFO question. I recognize a lot
is going on that I simply don't have the time or resources
to investigate. So I offer this record of my investigation as
part of a greater, ongoing effort by a body of tough-minded
scientists—some formally trained, some simply self-
taught—who seek to understand a phenomenon with
enormous significance for the world.

I've been involved only peripherally with close encounters of the fifth kind: abductions. Although my knowledge
is secondhand, limited to reading books such as Budd Hopkins's *Intruders* and talking with him and many abductees,
the subject itself ties in with my own perspective. According to the abductees, the aliens are attempting to crossbreed

with us to produce a mutant species. Why, we can only guess.

But to return to my own story, let's consider the indications that aliens are mining our planet. I have corroborating accounts from around this nation and from others, so my conclusion does not stand unsupported. (I'm still looking for the entrances to these underground alien bases, but haven't been successful yet.) But mining seems to be only one element in their mission.

Another involves the mutilation of cattle and other animals. ''Mutes''—animals whose various parts are removed with surgical precision—have been found dead in many parts of the middle and western United States. They have been associated with UFOs by people who've seen craft and/or lights at the sites and, in a few cases, even claim to have seen craft and aliens capturing cattle and disposing of them. The first animal mutilation case was noted about 1974. Since then the phenomenon of mysteriously mutilated animals has spread eastward; recently it reached the south shore of Long Island.

Often the dead cattle are found to have been drained of all blood. If the aliens are slaughtering cattle and other animals for blood and organs, I must conclude they are doing it for reasons so critical that it must mean life or death for them.

In support of this theory, I point to recent work by Dr. Mario Feola, a professor of surgery at Texas Tech University's Health Sciences Center. His work shows that a solution containing the hemoglobin of cattle blood has potential use for human blood replacement and could be used in emergencies if no human blood were available.

The human factor must be multifaceted. Here's the way I see it:

The first aspect of our role for the aliens is close encounters. Every encounter seems staged. A person appears to get exactly what he or she needs as proof or incentive to spread the word about UFOs.

The second aspect is the medical exam given to abductees aboard craft. Hopkins's research shows that abductees may be part of a genetic experiment in which, during the exam, a device is implanted in them. This small, BB-like object, only two or three millimeters in diameter, is inserted in the brain through the nostril with an instrument that looks like a large needle. The operation causes nosebleeds, which sometimes recur in people for years or during a later abduction when the implant is removed. Research indicates that abductees generally have more than one abduction. The first seems to occur in early childhood; others follow in adolescence and early adulthood.

If this research is valid—and I have no reason to doubt it—we have to ask many questions. How many people must the aliens examine to achieve their purpose? Are they tagging us like laboratory animals? Are we prey? Property? Do the aliens know compassion? Why do they disregard human feelings and our sense of respect for a person's right to freedom from coercion and bodily invasion?

The third aspect leads to even more significant implications. Some abductees report that while they were aboard the ships, humanlike beings who appeared to be working in concert with the aliens were also present. In some instances, these beings appeared only after an abductee became hysterical and out of control, as though the aliens felt that the abductee would be pacified by another human presence.

What are such humans or humanoids doing on a spacecraft full of aliens? Are they from this planet or somewhere else? If they are natives of earth, who are they and how were they recruited? If they are from elsewhere—the aliens' home planet, some off-world site where they were raised, a base on the moon or Mars, or a gigantic mother ship?—they could also be walking around our own planet at this very moment, having infiltrated human society. They could even have risen to high levels in every human institution, from which they could wield power to manipulate society in subtle, covert ways to suit the aliens' purpose. They could be invaders of the most dangerous kind—indistinguishable from true humans, yet entirely alien in their aims.

All of this is conjecture, and to dispel paranoia, indications are that real aliens cannot breathe our atmosphere for long. How long is unknown to me. But several sources, including some abductees, report that people have trouble breathing while aboard the ships. By implication, then, the aliens breathe something that is not identical with earth's atmosphere. Some of the human-looking aliens have been seen wearing spacesuits with helmets, as in the Travis Walton case. On the other hand, if the humanlike aliens are indeed truly human (but raised by the aliens from infancy and therefore mentally alien), we're right back to our scenario of indistinguishable invaders in top positions throughout the world.

The bottom line seems to be: aliens are here on a multifaceted mission, and none of it seems intended for human good (as in beneficial for individuals or our race).

The impression that their behavior is sinister is strengthened by the many UFO data that appear to be leaked from classified government and military sources, as if the aliens are in contact with certain elements of those institutions. Moreover, there is a distinct sense of disinformation to some of the data. The Majestic Twelve or MJ-12 situation, which alleges military retrieval of a crashed UFO and four dead aliens near Roswell, New Mexico, in 1947 (an event widely publicized, including a *New York Times* article and a discussion by Ted Koppel on *Nightline*) is a prime example. It appears that the public's knowledge about UFOs is being deliberately manipulated by sources whose purpose must therefore be suspect. How and where did the government and military get such data? Why release the information by leaking it to certain filmmakers, authors, and researchers? What's going on here?

I believe at least one secret group—perhaps stemming from MJ-12, perhaps parallel but separate from it—acts like a government within the government. Others have named it the secret establishment—the Trilateral Commission, the Bilderbergers, and/or "the illuminati." Its purpose seems to be world domination through all the institutions of human culture. Its shadowy powers reach out through the legitimate government and the military, through international finance, science, industry, education, even religion. It manipulates public opinion and world events so as to distract attention from its covert operations to consolidate political and economic powers for itself.

I had begun to think in terms of an underground government long before I ever heard the expression "illuminati." In fact, it was because I mentioned to some people that I suspected such an overt, but unknown, power elite that I was told of the illuminati conspiracy to establish a one-world government and social order. However, the facts are so vague and elusive that the illuminati concept seems more like a paranoid fantasy than a sociopolitical reality. Only in the light of exposures such as the Iran-Contra affair does it become clear that such conspiracies are not only possible but also likely. And if such a group exists, it would undoubtedly be the first to know of alien contact and would seek to control that knowledge for its own secret ends.

As for Big Brother watching us do research, I have several things to say. As we watch UFOs flying around Pine Bush and other parts of the world and as we publish books and articles about our findings, it would be most unlikely if we weren't being watched. I almost feel a comfort in knowing that someone has taken an interest in what we're doing. It means we're on target.

Now, no one has come knocking on my door demanding that I hand over information. My telephone seems to be bothered at times with strange noises and disconnects when I'm talking about bottom line information. In fact, it was through a mixup that I discovered who was playing the telephone game with me. I won't say how the mixup occurred and I won't give you the name of the group, but I will tell you its initials: C.I.A.

When I told Dale my thoughts, she said I'd hit the nail on the head. I said that my phone was "bothered with extra ears" and we equated it with the government communications van that monitored household conversations in the movie *ET: The Extraterrestrial*. Thereafter I was always on the lookout for strange vans and cars parked where they shouldn't have been. I could feel someone on the phone line, in addition to the phone noises, yet I never saw out-of-place cars or vans. One day Dale happened to look out the back windows of my house and saw the apartment complex nearby. She said to me, "You fool! They're not riding around in a van. They must have rented an apartment to watch you."

I was shocked. The thought had never occurred to me, but it seemed correct. I checked into monitoring equipment and was amazed to find that technology was available to monitor telephones without physical access to the lines, so that no one would ever know unless the spy made a mistake, which is exactly what happened.

But aside from the invasion of my privacy, I'm not worried about the spying group finding out what I know. I want everyone to know. I am looking for souvenirs—something tangible, something solid I can walk away with from Pine Bush or anywhere else. Humanity has a right to know at least some of what is going on. I believe the knowledge would change our consciousness, bringing planet earth a realistic sense of the cosmos. We would know as a race that we are not alone, and perhaps then we would behave more humanely to one another.

However, I must admit that result isn't inevitable, judging from the behavior of the secret establishment that undoubtedly has this knowledge already. And another aspect to the situation is even more frightening. One evening in California I was sitting around the courtyard pool with a group of people—our usual routine. On this occasion a man entered the courtyard and walked right to us. He had a stocky build and was dressed in a long-sleeved, tight-fitting black shirt and black pants. I'm not saying he was one of the so-called Men in Black, those sinister figures who many ufologists have written about, although he may have been. At the time, however, I simply considered it strange to be dressed that way in summer, even for California.

The man stared at all of us, particularly me. I wanted to ask him if he needed help, but everyone stopped talking, so I felt reluctant to speak. Besides, I was getting strange vibes from the guy.

For what seemed a minute or so, he simply stared at us. He never said a word, and then he turned around and left. Everyone started talking at once, yelling at each other for not questioning him. Apparently everyone had gotten an uneasy feeling from him. Looking back at the incident, I now think there was a connection with the ships I watched there. It's possible the man was nothing more than a crazy street person, but I think his action was too deliberate for that explanation. Perhaps he may, have been under some sort of control.

Scientists and ufologists who were involved in direct observations of UFOs told me that the small humanoids appeared to be biologically engineered rather than the original life form native to another planet. The small close encounter aliens were perfect for what they seemed to be doing. They were small and light; their huge eyes made them ideal for their nighttime work.

Many sizes and several types of eyes have been reported on the aliens. Large, solid black eyes have been reported over the last few years, since Whitley Strieber's *Communion* featured such an alien on the cover, but the alien I saw, like many others reported then, had eyes that were mostly yellow. The eyes reported on aliens prior to the all-black type varied from large and round to the wrap-around kind I saw at Pine Bush. I suspect the all-black type is actually a device over the eye, like a contact lens.

In addition to indications from others about biologically

engineered entities, my two photographs of aliens showed five quite different beings. Several of them look robotic, complete with rabbit ear antennae. Robots are built by someone. So if both the small humanoids and robots are manufactured, the logical question to ask is: who is doing the manufacturing and why? Are we again back to a "human" race, a master race, perhaps?

Suppose an underground government or secret power elite is running this planet—or attempting to—and an alien race arrived here and began to monitor civilization to discover who the real rulers are. Once they had that information, the aliens would be able to solicit help from them for their mission. They could tune in to who and where these ruling people are, as well as learn what is going on.

However, if the aliens can get from "there" to "here," couldn't they help themselves? What kind of aliens would need help from humans? Robots wouldn't need help, nor would biologically manufactured units. So we're back to the question of who's running the show. I assume that aliens, especially if some of them looked human, could and would, if they are able to travel to earth, be able also to go after their goal here fairly easily.

But what if the aliens are a dying race? Something seems to be monumentally wrong with the way they're doing things, which leads me to conclude that they face a life or death situation. It is a situation in which they have to go about their business secretly. In fact, that conclusion leads to only one possibility and to save themselves they may have to do something extreme to us.

On the other hand, if they are relatively human in form, as they seem to be, they may be here to seek a cure for their fatal problem. Since cattle blood shows potential for replacing human blood in some situations, perhaps the cattle mutilations are due to the aliens using cattle blood as one approach to revitalizing their race, such as in nurturing fetuses.

Another approach seems to involve genetic experiments

and an interspecies breeding program. Some abductees, according to Budd Hopkins, have seen babies that the aliens say are the abductees' offspring, raised by the aliens. Intuitively, the abductees sense that to be true, even though the babies have a look that is partly alien, partly human. Now, on our planet, species cannot crossbreed with another. For example, chimpanzees, our closest relatives, are genetically closed to breeding with humans. You can cross a horse with a donkey to get a mule, but mules are always sterile and cannot reproduce. If the aliens have been crossbreeding with us, they are either genetically linked with us, probably as ancestors from a remote past, or they know how to manipulate genetic material from us. They may be close relatives, biologically speaking. The logical conclusion, then, is that the aliens originated on earth or that we humans originated elsewhere—in the aliens' territory—and were "seeded" here, as in the panspermia theory proposed by prominent scientists, including astronomer Fred Hoyle and molecular biologist Francis Crick.

This is speculation, of course—theory—yet it is not unfounded theory. Sometimes it's necessary to speculate in order to progress. Science speculates by proposing testable hypotheses. In this case, the hypothesis is not yet testable, but it does make for a thought experiment in logic and analysis, using the data we have. Some may criticize these theories as unbridled fantasy; let them. My quest is to know the truth about what is going on and why I have been personally—and unwillingly—brought into something quite bizarre and contrary to everything we believe and take for reality.

Since the aliens have come secretly and silently, they may have infiltrated humanity on every level, invading earth on a life-or-death mission. Some people might object by saying the aliens are here to save us. We are a doomed race, such people say, because of the threat of nuclear war and environmental destruction by our own hands, and the aliens are here for our good. If that is the case, I say the aliens have done everything wrong thus far.

Coming to this planet under cover to dig on people's private farmland is not "good." Nor is it good to terrify the residents of farms and homes so that they stay inside at night, afraid to venture out. Likewise, it is not good to buzz commercial airliners in flight, causing pilots to take emergency action to avoid a midair crash.

Even worse, the close encounters people have had leave them with terrible aftereffects, and for the most part, they are traumatized. The encounters have not been good for the frightened people. The people, when they've had the courage to speak publicly of their encounters, have most often met skepticism and ridicule, which leads to further mental anguish.

No, the aliens are not here for our good. In fact, it appears that just the opposite is true. The aliens are deliberately confusing things to ensure we have no clear picture of what is occurring. They're hiding something. And with their technology, they can do just about anything to anyone, any time, any place—no holds barred. The only trouble is, they appear to recognize that we humans won't approve of it.

Having come to these conclusions as a result of logical analysis, I have to add that my emotions are not in complete agreement. When I am with people in the fields and woods of the Pine Bush area chasing the ships, we are drawn to them without a sense of overwhelming evil awaiting us. Generally speaking, I feel people are not continually drawn toward evil, especially when emotions run high with fear and everyone is tuning in to the ships on psychic as well as physical levels. People wouldn't be drawn to the aliens time after time if the aliens demonstrated obvious bad intentions; their "bad vibes" would be felt strongly enough to warn people away. I certainly wouldn't chase them if I felt something bad coming from them or if I felt I were in danger. I must admit, however, that on occasion there have been vibes so powerful that they affected my solar plexus.

Other people have been affected likewise on those occasions. What was going on, we could only guess. But whenever I've felt such bad vibes, I've taken the hint and left.

If it sounds like I have a love-hate relationship with the aliens, you're close to correct. I don't hate them, but I do have a deep-seated suspicion. At the same time, I have an honest feeling of emotional warmth toward them. Soon after I began interacting with the ships at Pine Bush, I had to look deeply into myself to find out what was going on. I was shocked to discover that I felt love from them and I was returning it. Almost every encounter, despite the fear, felt good to me (except for those occasional bad vibes). Sure, I've been angry at the aliens and frustrated because I don't understand what they're doing and why, and because I don't like to be manipulated and mocked. But I've never felt genuine hostility coming either from them or from me.

With all my antics in trying to read them, it is as if they thought I was funny, knowing I was trying to make contact and preventing it, avoiding me by remaining invisible except where it suited their purposes to show themselves. It sometimes has taken me an hour to get into a field where I thought they were. Just as I'd arrive, they would take off and fly overhead on their merry way or they would freeze and remain invisible. Now, when the field is fifty acres and you're on foot, you can't check every inch of it in an evening. So I'd wait, and after an hour or so, I'd leave, frustrated. Just as I'd get back to the road, I'd see a craft lift up from where I'd been and move over the tree line to another field. Or—and this just infuriated me—it would fly by and acknowledge my effort. Thus far I've focused on the physical reality of the ships, aliens, and abductions. But what about the psychic dimension? Are we dealing with a race of psychic beings? Has there been psychic contact between aliens and people?

I realized many years ago I could do things mentally that other people apparently couldn't. I've lived with it every day and have used this power to help me understand things.

When the ships entered my life, people told me that psychic powers have a lot to do with contacting them. My experience made me disagree. "No, something else has to do with contact," I'd say. What that something else is, remains to be seen.

Metaphysical teachings thousands of years old tell us that everyone has spirit guides watching over us to guide us in our journey through life toward that which is best for the growth of our souls. Many people can tune in to the guides, communicating directly with them and receive data and instruction from them. This process is called channeling, which I accept as a real phenomenon. It certainly is widely associated with the UFO experience. I won't give a discourse on it here for the skeptics or the nonbelievers; there are many books on the subject, including Jon Klimo's book *Channeling*, which presents the full range of research and opinion about the reality of the phenomenon.

In my judgment, many people don't know what they are channeling. They assume they are tuning in to aliens when in reality they are contacting their own spirit guides or even what metaphysics calls the higher self—a level of awareness even beyond spirit guides. In all my experience of observing the aliens and bringing talented psychics to Pine Bush to attempt to contact the aliens, none of us were able to channel the aliens. In fact, several psychics who tried were surprised to learn that something like a wall of energy surrounds the aliens, protecting them from any attempts to reach them on the psychic level, whether through telepathy, clairvoyance, or astral projection.

Guides talk to people but the aliens remain silent, so far as I've experienced. I therefore doubt the reality of claims by psychics who say they're channeling beings from the Pleiades, Arcturus, another galaxy, etc. Over the years I've tried every type of contact with the aliens, from psychic communications and meditation to astral projections. Nothing has worked.

I therefore conclude that the aliens have the technological

means to isolate themselves even from psychic contact! Their science has given them a profound understanding of energies beyond those that human science recognizes—or rather is just beginning to recognize through the pioneering work of Nikola Tesla and more recent physicists working on the fringes of science who are following his lead. The aliens have technologically ''bottled'' psychic abilities.

Consider this. Abductees who have remembered their experiences without the aid of hypnosis have described being caught in beams of light projected either from the aliens' ships or from hand-held instruments. The beams have varied in color. The aliens seem to use specific colors during different phases of the abduction process. Sequences of colors seem to cause different physical sensations in the abductees.

There have also been cases where aliens not only came right through the walls of houses, but also took their unwilling victims back with them the same way. But this strange dematerialization isn't complete. In the case of Betty Andreasson, the aliens told her to move some loose china on a window sill because it would get in the way when they returned through the wall. Weird and doubly weird. Yet it makes more sense to interpret that incident as a limitation of technology than as a purely mental ability.

I believe, therefore, that the aliens can communicate telepathically, perceive clairvoyantly (what parapsychologists now call remote viewing), and even astrally project themselves and humans—all on the basis of technology. Earlier I noted that this phenomenon is called psychotronics. I would describe the aliens as a psychotronic society, just as we are a mechanized/electronic society.

When I became aware of the Tesla field effect, I wanted to know what would happen if my colleagues and I came upon a Tesla field as we walked through a cornfield or pasture. Would we be able to tell it was there? Would we bump into it? How would it feel? Would it repel us in some manner?

I put my questions to electronics experts. I was told that entering a Tesla field would probably feel like electrical raindrops on the skin.

If the aliens have attained the technological means to accomplish what we humans think of as psychic powers, they may be able to accomplish a range of things, from tuning in someone's thoughts through devices to eavesdropping on conversations to remote sensing of a person's bodily functions. I've seen evidence of alien responses to people's voiced wishes or feelings, including my own. On the other hand, I've never seen evidence of genuine mind reading. I've tried to trick the aliens many times to see if they could read my mind and anticipate what I was going to do next, but they have never been successful when I make a snap decision to deviate from my usual behavior. They react based on knowledge of my prior behavior, even though it's inappropriate because of my last minute change of plan.

As for telepathy, many people say they've experienced telepathic communications from the aliens and it feels different from human telepathy. It feels like a radio is being blasted into their heads—sometimes too loudly. Improper volume control seems to me more like a mechanical problem than a psychic connection. It seems the aliens are using electronics that link up to biology—i.e., psychotronics.

Another aspect of the psychic dimension is the aura, which is an energy envelope surrounding the living body. The envelopes or "clouds" include both physical forms of energy (such as electromagnetism) and nonphysical (such as etheric). The colors, brightness, and density of a person's aura, it is said by psychics, reflect that person's physical, mental, emotional, and spiritual condition. (Kirlian photography offers supporting evidence with the electromagnetic energy field revealed in Kirlian photographs.) A colleague believes that the aliens have the capability to see the human aura and to understand many things about people by translating characteristics of their aura into psychophysical terms. For example, someone who's likely to be a good candidate for alien abduction might be selected on the basis of auric colors that indicate an emotional state the aliens consider best for their purposes.

But the reverse would also be true. If humans have auras, so would aliens. So would the humanoids created by the aliens and so would the true humans raised by the aliens. Psychics who see auras may possibly determine the validity of my hypothesis if a different type of aura becomes noticeable around people. Such people may be, emotionally speaking, aliens—and perhaps even psychophysiologically speaking as well.

# CHAPTER 15

• • •

# THE PHOTOGRAPHS—AND ALL UFO PHOTOGRAPHS

I HAVE TRIED to use the scientific method in this field work. The scientific method is basically the following process: collection of data, analysis, publication of findings and conclusions, and peer review. In controlled experiments, data should be repeatable; in field investigation, it's catch-as-catch-can. And the aliens and their craft are extremely hard to catch! Photography introduces some degree of repeatability to the situation because others have taken photos similar to mine.

In fact, all the basic images and situations of ships that I've photographed have been replicated by others, more than once. The images are consistent; clearly a coherent process is at work that any competent observer can investigate. My photos are not the result of darkroom mistakes, dirt or lint on a negative, lens flares, or anything other than alien craft.

Photographs have been the key piece of evidence in human attempts to solve the UFO enigma because they objectify what our eyes see. Photographs have also been the most frustrating obstacle to reaching a solution because of hoaxes and unclear shots taken by technically ignorant people. Photography is a double-edged sword for ufologists. Everyone keeps hoping for a definitive photo—the clear-cut "real" picture of a craft in the sky. I understand and share those hopes, but after photographing the ships in a systematic manner for so many years, I've made startling discoveries that indicate those hopes are in vain. Those in the know—i.e., the government intelligence community—apparently discovered it before I did but kept their knowledge a secret.

When I took my initial photographs in 1971—using a 35mm camera set at f/2.8 with a shutter speed of 1/60 of a second—we all saw clearly visible metallic-looking UFOs, but the pictures showed cloudy blue vapors streaming off the UFO that we hadn't seen.

In 1978, when I took an aerial photography course, I brought in prints of my slides to show the professor. He took one look and started to yell, "Oh, my God. . . . What is this? You were too close to something giving off ultraviolet radiation! What is this?" Startled by his reaction, I told him what they were and he was stunned. For me, it marked the beginning of a growing realization that scientists trained in scientific photography and those who know shortwave radiation photographs—people involved in photographing nuclear reactor processes—would have clear, precise knowledge of what was occurring in photographs.

In 1980, when I began taking photographs in Pine Bush, I knew what I had seen. Four of us were standing next to a field while two cameras clicked away. We were looking at large triangle ships about two hundred feet in perimeter. But when the films came back from the developer, nothing was on them that resembled what we had seen. Instead of clear-cut triangle ships, there were exotic discharges and sprays of multicolored lights in a seemingly chaotic fashion. However, careful inspection showed that the lights seemed to begin where the outline of the craft should have been, apparently shooting out of vents at different parts of the craft. In some photos the outline was barely discernible. But why were the craft themselves not visible?

At first, everyone said the photos should be computer-enhanced. Computer enhancement is a process in which a computer scans a photograph so that every detail is displayed on the monitor. This process is most effectively done in black and white, although color imagery in computers continues to improve. The photos are digitized—that is, broken down into dots like a newspaper photo. Each dot can be enlarged. Most people have seen some aspect of computer enhancement through television coverage of the space program in which photos of distant planets are transmitted through radio waves back to earth. The Jet Propulsion Laboratory in Pasadena, California, apparently has the best equipment for computer enhancement, and JPL photos have often been used in media coverage of space probes, moon landings, and so forth.

Through computer enhancement, sections of a photograph can be enlarged and viewed as a complete image in themselves. Then otherwise vague details often become readily apparent. Computer enhancement is especially useful in detecting fraudulent photos of UFOs—of which there have been many. In the famous photos by Swiss contactee Eduard Meier, offered to the public first in the book *Contact from the Pleiades* and then naively supported by Gary Kinder in his examination of the Meier case entitled *Light Years,* a hoax was detected through computer enhancement. A private organization called Ground Saucer Watch, which specializes in photo evaluation and which has access to JPL's equipment, showed that the Meier photos of UFOs are really small models suspended by strings. Meier, it turns out, is a master modelmaker and computer enhanced photoanalysis showed the result of that skill.

Although computer enhancement works well for detecting phony photos and for authenticating genuine photos, its value is nevertheless limited. I didn't have my photos computer enhanced because I found that a well-made darkroom enlargement does a much better job of showing details. In a darkroom, there is more control if the print is especially uneven in dark and light tones. The computer's advantage is that scientists operate the computers, see firsthand what is occurring in the photo and can bring their expertise to the analysis.

A year after I had taken the photos but still didn't know what was in them, I met a photographer who told me to enlarge the color negatives in black and white. Since I have my own darkroom, that process posed no problem. I planned to enlarge every detail in all of the initial fourteen photographs. I was never concerned that anything I was doing had to be proven to anyone else. I took the photos and wanted to know exactly what I had photographed—it was as simple as that. I wasn't out to make money from UFO research. I wanted to do that with my music, not with something I considered due to chance or mere luck.

So there I was in my darkroom, at two o'clock in the morning, staring in disbelief at the first enlargement. Two figures appeared to be standing beside the craft. But it couldn't be! Yes, we had seen the ships on the ground. Yes, I had taken a number of pictures of them on the ground. Yes, I had assumed someone was driving them. And, yes, I knew I had registered on film what we didn't actually see with our eyes.

But aliens in my photos? I couldn't believe it.

I made an acetate tracing of the photo. The details screamed out at me. I went on to the next photo. I wanted to look at a number of details.

About four o'clock in the morning a terrible feeling passed through me. Five aliens were visible in the second photo, plus the structure of the craft. Four were standing inside the area of the ''light spray''; one was beside the craft. The two aliens from the first picture were also in the second, which was taken three frames later (perhaps five minutes apart). I traced the second photo also and then, feeling physically and mentally exhausted, I cleaned up and went to bed.

The next day I showed the photos to Harry. As he touched the first one, a wave of ''something'' passed over him. He said, ''I just got a really weird feeling.'' He described it and what he described was exactly what I had felt when I first enlarged the photos. We were feeling alien energy. The photo seemed to have captured more than just an image of the aliens. Their energy seemed attached to the visual image. As I said, I have felt it many times since. It has such an immediate and powerful effect on me that I named one of my electronic music compositions "Alien Energy" as a way of expressing musically some of what I experienced. Alien energy or alien vibes are very different from a human's. We are so accustomed to each other's vibrations/energy/auras as a race that most often we don't even notice them, and instead function strictly on the basis of physical-sensory data. But the aliens have a different energy vibration than we do. It's a thick, dense, very physical feeling that unnerves people. People accompanying me on my nighttime jaunts have felt it as fear or "creepy vibes" as I have stated previously.

When I enlarged the other photos, several of them had portions of the ships in them, but no aliens were visible. The black and white enlargements proved to be the best way to bring out details. I used high contrast paper and began making 14" × 17" enlargements to bring out the smallest details.

Then I realized I had a critical decision to make. What should I tell people about the photos when I showed them? Should I mention the beings? Should I describe them or point them out? Would that be leading people? Should I say anything at all? It was sensational enough simply to say I had photographed some UFOs when I wasn't trying to be sensational—only investigatory. If I told people I had photographed aliens as well, it might seem totally preposterous. I'd already met enough derision from certain people over my field trips to know that I didn't want any more. So, feeling that discretion is the better part of valor, I decided to say nothing and just play it by ear.

As I showed the photographs to experts in physics, commercial photography, scientific photography, and the media,

I was surprised and disappointed to realize how prejudiced
people are about the idea of UFOs. Even before they looked
at my photos, they were expressing disbelief. Everyone had
something to say about the subject, and it was usually negative. I avoided arguments. I simply said that opinions—
theirs and mine alike—didn't matter at this point because
so few data exist. I just wanted to know what was in the
photos, and if they could help me with that quest, fine.

I listened to everything, even when it was obviously way
off course. Sometimes the most innocent or the most ob-
noxious remark offered a perspective I hadn't thought of.
However, only when I began talking with scientists involved with radiation physics did I gain some understanding. I learned some fascinating facts about phenomena
above and below the human threshold of vision.

The human eye can see in the visible portion of the electromagnetic radiation spectrum, which spans roughly 400
to 700 nanometers (nm). This is the range of visible light.
Shortwave radiation is radiation from about 1 to 400 nm.
The shorter wavelengths in this range are ultraviolet, x-rays,
and gamma rays. Longer wavelengths—those above 700
nm—consist of infrared, microwaves, television, and radio
waves. The Kodak company's technical pamphlets on the
many fields of scientific photography, and the technical
specifications of the film, proved to be the critical factors
in determining what was apparently occurring in the photographs.

From my reading and conversations, I learned that all
film sold over the counter is sensitive to shortwave radiation. I deduced that the sprays or bursts of light appearing
in my photos must be due to shortwave radiation between
what our eyes see and what the film is sensitive to. The
ships had been discharging shortwave radiation. My eyes
couldn't see it but my camera and film did.

Physics textbooks state that any object surrounded by
ultraviolet light will, when photographed, be blurred on the
film. This fact dovetailed with other things I knew more

generally. Some people claim to have been sunburned by UFOs. The point was made plainly in *Close Encounters of the Third Kind* when Richard Dreyfuss's character, Roy Neary, comes home after his first close encounter to find that half his face is reddened. Shortwave radiation was responsible.

Two distinctly different types of spray appeared in my photographs. One was a sort of zipper effect, probably resulting from an alternating current. The other looked like globules, sometimes misshapen.

By chance I saw a television program on solar and astrophotography. I was surprised that x-ray photographs of the sun showed elements similar to what I had in some of my photos. In fact, the similarity seemed so strong that I wanted to show them to an astronomer. Eventually, I showed them to several astronomers. They agreed independently that certain elements were the same as what x-rays of the sun showed.

X-ray emissions from the sun occur in greatly fluctuating magnetic regions. The bright points are known as "tight loop" formations. The loops are too bright to show up in detail in a general picture. Special equipment must be used to photograph the loops so that details are observable. The active magnetic region causes flares in a variety of colors, such as my film registers—all invisible to my eyes. The odd shapes of the bright globules or chunks of light that I designate as my second type of spray may be caused by a bipolar field, which is highly fluctuating and thus distorts the shape.

Ultraviolet light shows up as bluish bursts in photographs, as well as causing an object to blur. When I read this information in a textbook, I looked over my photos. Every one of the original set has a bluish globule-type of lightburst. Some of my prints from Fotomat had a darkened background, so I asked to have them printed lighter. When I received the new prints, the bursts were there.

Harry had received two photographs from someone who

said they were daytime shots of a UFO. They showed sprays "dripping" through the sky and faint blue bursts of light. We went through the many UFO books on the market, looking at the photos, and discovered there were many like mine showing x-ray emissions and ultraviolet radiation. We realized that if anyone had simply compared the many photographs against the technical specifications of film, he or she could have easily discovered what was going on.

Another fact emerged from this photographic evaluation—an even more startling revelation—and again it was logically deduced from the film evidence and a simple knowledge of physics. The sun uses fusion power. I reasoned that if the ships were producing x-ray emissions from magnetic fields in my photos, and *if* solar characteristics were exhibited in other people's photos from around the world, then *the aliens were using fusion to power their craft.* It would have to be an incredibly sophisticated system, I felt, considering the fact that our own fusion research program, principally carried on at Princeton University and the University of Rochester, was still so primitive that it had yet to sustain a fusion reaction, let alone produce it in a technology that could be introduced into small aircraft as a power source.

It may even be the case—and I say this only speculatively—that the psychic dimension of the UFO experience involves properties of electromagnetism not yet controlled or understood by humans. For example, the aliens seem to communicate telepathically with abductees. However, thanks to the research of Budd Hopkins and others, it now appears that the telepathy involves the small BB-like device described earlier. The device is implanted in abductees' brains to act as a transceiver. Radio waves, of course, are a form of electromagnetism. Moreover, many contactees tell of being immobilized by aliens who shoot a beam of light at them from a handheld device. John White calls it a "kundalini gun" because its effects on the person mimic some of the more superficial effects long noted in the kundalini phenomenon. He says the aliens use it to manipulate the human nervous system, inducing pseudomystical feelings that for the naive person—most abductees—can be used to psychologically addict or imprint them to the situation in which the kundalini gun is used. (Ufologist John Keel gives the fullest description of this phenomenon in *The Mothman Prophecies*. White's basic text about the subject is *Kundalini, Evolution and Enlightenment*.) Light, too, is a form of electromagnetism.

These apparently distinct pieces of data indicate more generally that the aliens use electromagnetism with incredible proficiency, probably in ways that, when we understand them, will rationalize much that we presently relegate to the realm of the psychic and the paranormal.

Photographs taken by a number of people with me in Pine Bush, and by others in quite different situations, support my conclusions. In 1983, I was in a bar with some musician friends. One of the men in the group asked me to take a picture of his band with his polaroid camera. He handed me the camera but then took it back, saying he wanted to take a picture of a waitress's legs first. He snapped one photo and handed me the camera. As he handed it to me, it suddenly flashed off another picture. We looked at the camera and it flashed off a third picture. Neither of us had our hands anywhere near the button.

When the pictures developed, everyone stared at the images. There were pairs of colored curving lines coming off the waitress's legs in the first photo—almost identical to the discharge or spray photos I'd taken of the UFOs. The second picture showed her walking away with a ghostly mist behind her and three pairs of short, curved lines looking as if they were coming after her. The third photo showed the curved lines in a different pattern.

The waitress looked at them and was very upset. I attempted to calm her and I told her that sometimes, when highly emotional events occur in a person's life, they give rise to strange physical effects. That might explain these photos, I said. We just happened to have the camera there and you were subconsciously dealing with something emotional, I told her, and the mental energy associated with the emotions manifested itself onto film. The waitress confirmed what I'd surmised. She was going through a divorce, she said, and was falling apart emotionally. She had no idea about the physics of the situation that might result in such photos, but my assessment of the situation seemed to reassure her.

A 1984 incident also bears on this situation. My friend and colleague, Cathy McCartney, took a picture that provided the first occasion for us to even consider whether there were some sort of psychic occurrences in connection with the UFOs.

We had been standing in the cemetery and she aimed her camera at some white lights flying by. When she got the developed film back, the photo was so similar to my polaroids that we were amazed. Streams of curved, multicolored lines were paired off in all directions. There are several different types of detailed lines in the photo—all against the black sky. We recalled what was happening when she took the picture. I had snapped some shots then, but I must have snapped them at a slightly different time.

We still don't know whether the dribbled lines are small and located directly over her and the camera, or whether they are large and farther away. But why they should have been there at all is the mystery.

People who are familiar with parapsychological research may assume that I was involved with thoughtography or psychic photography and that I was the unwitting agent behind the photos. It seems that some people have the psychic ability, conscious or otherwise, to precipitate images and forms onto photographic film. This subject of thoughtography has been investigated by a number of parapsychologists; a useful survey can be found in *Psychic Exploration* by Apollo 14 astronaut Edgar D. Mitchell.

However, based on my reason, research, and personal experience and especially my photographic evidence—I must say that I reject the idea that I, either alone or in combination with a friend or friends, was the source of the lightforms appearing on film. I could accept that an emotionally distraught waitress in the presence of several psychic people could cause emotional tension sufficient to precipitate the colored streamers. But why did similar markings appear in Cathy's Pine Bush photos while we stood calmly looking at ships that we didn't even clearly see at the time? I believe the aliens have developed a technological means of producing phenomena that we conventionally term psychic. In other words, they've bottled psychic power. I know that genuine psychic phenomena occur between humans, but I do not believe the aliens can read my mind without aid from equipment. I believe they are tapping into the same realm as people who have psychic abilities. Their technology allows them to open a doorway to our minds, so to speak, which in turn allows them to produce events we call psychic phenomena. How that is accomplished, I can't say, but it seems to involve either control of energies unknown to us or remarkable control of conventional energies in a way we have not yet understood. Some people, especially contactees, declare that aliens are a psychic race. If so, why do they fly around in metallic ships constructed with nuts and bolts? If they are psychic beings, they'd have no need for such craft.

In 1984, I realized that my photos needed a ground reference, so I tried using my flash to light up the foreground, not the ships. This technique proved successful. Fences, grass, roadsides, foliage—whatever's there is fine for identifying the exact location of the photograph. Now my colleagues and I all use flash.

## TESLA FIELDS AND UNSEEN BEAMS

The first image of a Tesla field appeared in my photos in 1984; all others date from 1986 and after. Other people have also photographed Tesla fields. When I started photographing Tesla fields and reading about psychotronic research, I became convinced that the UFOs used an advanced form of fusion power. Dale had told me that Tesla fields have two characteristic shapes: One is round or globelike; the other is football-shaped. Some have a flattened section, like a balloon being pressed onto the ground. The ones I've photographed vary in size from a tennis ball to a house. Bearden, of course, describes them as being larger than cities when used as defensive shields against missiles. Not long after Dale told me about the fields, I saw both shapes in my photographs. One picture in particular had an enormous football-shaped Tesla field standing on its end in the middle of a cornfield. It seemed to be fairly near where I was standing.

At one point Tesla fields began to show up in many of my photographs, both in the sky and on the ground. I soon saw that the force fields appeared to have different densities, ranging from opaque through a milky translucence to nearly transparent. Many of them were bigger than a house. One photo shows several globular Tesla fields during early evening, when it was still light outside; in it, one transparent globe is clearly sitting atop a barn.

None of these were visible to unaided human eyes. I took the photographs either because I saw lights in the sky and snapped off a shot of the field unknowingly, or else I just went on vibes that led me to take a blind shot simply on the basis of feeling urgency. I now realize that feeling is physiological—an effect coming from the electrostatic Tesla fields that cause the hair on some people's skin to stand up, similar to the sensations just before lightning strikes close by.

In many of our Tesla photos, the energy field has a flat bottom, as if resting on something. Since it is not resting on treetops, there must be something else we can't see. Our

Tesla field photographs show large globes appearing to sit atop invisible columns.

The dense Tesla fields might even be generating a power source to enable some specific type of work to be done. The vertical invisible tunnel on which the Tesla globe rests might also be creating an environment to enable the aliens to work since some of them apparently can't breathe our atmosphere for more than a short time.

Another new development is photographing what looks like a "pole" or beam of light that no one saw when the shot was taken. The first photos of this phenomenon were taken by a woman in July 1987 and later that autumn. I got my first beam the following November, and now several other people have also photographed visually unperceived beams of light in the fields around Pine Bush. We were snapping off photos of craft, and were surprised to see the pictures showing beams of invisible light quite close to us. Because all of us were using flash, we captured the ground and foliage around the lightbeams and therefore could identify their exact location. With pictures in hand, we went to the sites to look.

One beam was next to a wire farm fence. The only oddity was that the photo showed a lightbeam sticking up seven feet or so almost directly in front of where we had been standing. Another of the beams went right through a tree next to the road. There could be no mistaking that we were photographing something belonging to someone else. Some of the beam photos also had Tesla fields in them. We took repeated pictures of the beams in the same places and other places as well—enough times to realize that the beams were apparently turned on and off. We never knew which mode they were in, of course, because we couldn't see them or sense them otherwise.

We showed our photographs to some physicists and electronics technicians. The consensus was that the beams were coming up from the ground, not down from the sky. All the beams were along roadsides, and we had been deep in the fields, for the most part, when we photographed them. Moreover, they were in key areas for the ships, as we were. We were sure that they had a very specific purpose.

Perhaps they were tracking beams or beacons for the ships. The beams could line the roads around the key fields and act as runway lights for approaching craft (into new areas or for new pilots coming to new areas). Coded beams could signify specific areas being worked on or in operation at a specific time. This interpretation would tie in with my conclusion about underground installations with monitoring devices to track humans.

Once again, I believe that the inability to photograph craft clearly is due to deliberate disturbance of the film's emulsion by the aliens. Such disturbances confuse people, who wonder how and why their cameras see something different from what their eyes see. Since the aliens seem to try to confuse things in every other way, this little stunt fits in perfectly with their *modus operandi*.

In fact, they seem so adept at this trickery that I imagine they've had considerable practice. They seem to know exactly how to do it because they've studied film chemistry and know its reactions to various stimuli. So much of what the aliens do is well-controlled and designed to confuse.

I am sure specialized equipment would enable me to take clear photographs of the craft in their full, physical form. Dale and Mark said special lenses had been constructed for government photographers to get clear moving film footage of the ships, as well as still photos. The film, I'm told, was spectacular.

But I never had the financial resources necessary to obtain proper equipment, and I still don't. I looked into the military equipment market and learned that the price of nighttime infrared goggles, which are given to soldiers in the field, is $6,500 a pair. My friends and I had a good laugh over that. I had nearly bankrupted myself to buy my $450 Nikon and an inexpensive telephoto lens.

In 1988, I met a research scientist, Paul Sher, from a

major corporation. After examining my photos, he decided I should try x-ray film that comes in individual sheets.

He started me off with four, 5×7-inch sheets of x-ray film. I was to use one film at a time for each sighting by holding each sheet up and waving it around every time I saw something I thought would register.

The results were significant enough for Paul to write the following details:

The films used for your experiment were Agfa-Gevaert, Osray M3, high speed/high contrast radiographic films. Developing time was 4½ minutes and fixing time was 5 minutes.

Results:

Film #1 was used as a control blank and no radiation was detected.

Film #2 was marked "Fri July 15, 1988, many ships flying at treelines about 1000' away." Developed film did not indicate any radiation.

Film #3 was marked "July 25, 1988, Monday, variety of lights, nothing visually significant." Developed film did not indicate any radiation.

Film #4 was marked "Friday August 19, 1988, 1 large thing twice, small lights." This developed film had some spots and small clusters dotted about the film. Since the films used were handheld, lacking any focused plane, there is no way of interpreting directions, geometric shapes, etc.

Take note that smudges produced from my fingerprints do not resemble the cluster of dots located on film #4.

I think that the results found are interesting enough to warrant further efforts with radiographic films. My suggestion would be to try several more films in exactly the same manner as these 4 submitted films. If any possible radiation is detected, perhaps you could try again using focused camera techniques.

I'm sorry that these films could not be printed, as the amount of information on the films was so slight that the contrast was insufficient for printing. (Paul Sher has spent almost three decades in the scientific field. His work in research has included such disciplines as electron-beam acceleration, infrared and nuclear magnetic resonance spectroscopy, and x-ray diffraction.)


## HOW TO PHOTOGRAPH A UFO

Since one purpose of this book is to encourage others to perform UFO photography, here are instructions based on trial-and-error over the years by my colleagues and me. Remember that you will not be dealing photographically with visible light from the ships and what you see is not what you'll get.

Use a good camera that allows manual control. I prefer a 35 mm. Some of the automatics give good results; some don't.

Set the shutter speed at about $\frac{1}{60}$ of a second (some cameras go only as slow as $\frac{1}{90}$ of second) and the aperture as wide open as possible. (My Nikon goes to f/1.4.) If you have especially steady hands, you might use $\frac{1}{30}$ of a second.

All film is sensitive to shortwave radiation. The faster-speed films—ASA 1000 and 1600—are too grainy for good quality. They can be used, but I prefer ASA 400. Use a flash—not to light the object but to light the foreground for reference. Try to get something identifiable, such as a fence, tree, bush, road sign, etc.

My colleagues and I have tried using Polaroids, hoping we would see immediately what we'd shot, but the results were disappointing. Polaroid film turned out to be the film worst suited to our purpose. It has limited camera flash range—about ten feet compared to perhaps thirty feet for other kinds—and the film is not sensitive to the short wavelengths the way 35mm film is, despite the ASA 600 claim.

After you've gotten your equipment, go into the field and experiment. Keep careful records. I carry a small cassette recorder to audiotape my voice; that way I can speak aloud to record what I'm seeing and any other pertinent information leaving my hands and eyes free to deal with the situation.

What about developing the film? I recommend that you use a "one hour commercial lab." I've tried many custom photo labs and had many problems. I've found the one-hour labs to be best. Tell the clerk you took nighttime shots of lights in the sky and you want every frame printed. Or you can tell them to develop just the negatives so that you can pick the frames you want to have printed.

# CHAPTER 16

• • •

# A DISCUSSION OF
# SELECTED PHOTOGRAPHS

THE PHOTOGRAPHS REPRODUCED here are just a few of
the nine hundred-plus photographs of UFOs I've taken
since 1971.

In general, two distinct types of discharges are displayed
spraying off different portions of the ships. The discharges
are invisible and make it virtually impossible to clearly
photograph the craft with a normal glass lens. The data I've
given here are based on what was seen, what the film can
and did register, and the transmission qualities of the glass
lens. (As far as I know, all UFO photographs have been
blurred except for hoaxes.)

*Type One Discharge.* The first type of discharge appears
to be an electrical alternating current spurting off areas of
the craft, either horizontally or vertically. This discharge is
apparently due to an electromagnetic field that surrounds
the craft (and could cause ionization).

*Type Two Discharge.* The second type of discharge comprises several different types of sprays of short-wave radiation emissions. This discharge has clumps or pieces of
lights floating in the air. These clumps exhibit characteristic
traits of x-ray emissions and bipolar, highly fluctuating
magnetic fields. Compactness of the field produces unre-
solvable clumping or tight loop formations unless further
specialized equipment can be utilized. Fluctuations in this

magnetic field could be responsible for the colorations in various flares of emissions. When astronomer Robert Jastrow at Columbia University saw some of my early photographs, he commented, "I'm unable to interpret these images as atmospheric electricity. They may be something totally unknown to us at this time."

**1.** POD MARK. *Taken:* July 1985 of a depression in the ground made on March 30 or 31, 1985.

The depression began at about five inches deep and eroded to a shallower depth. It was directly behind the fence of the Jewish cemetery, dating from the event described in chapter 8. Some small rocks are scattered about in the pod mark. During the four months between the event and the photo, weeds had grown around the pod mark but nothing had grown in it.

**2.** ANOTHER POD MARK. *Taken:* September 1985 of a depression made earlier that year.

The depression measured two feet by three feet, as if a giant egg was pressed into the ground. The bottom of the depression is eroded to a flat surface about six inches below ground level. Apparently, the ships' landing gear releases radiation into the soil. The grass dies and nothing will grow in it for months to years. This pod mark remained approximately the same from the time we found it for more than two years. At that time the cemetery staff dug up the spot and planted grass in it.

**3.** LARGE MULTICOLORED TESLA FIELD ON THE GROUND. *Taken:* September 9, 1986 at Pine Bush, New York. *Camera:* Nikon 35mm SLR with 50mm lens. *Film:* Kodacolor negative print film (ASA 400). *Exposure:* $\frac{1}{60}$ sec. at f/1.4 with flash.

I was riding along a road at night when I saw lights above the trees. I took a flash picture and continued to a spot I commonly use for observation. I was shocked when I saw the photo developed.

The road can be seen at the bottom right, showing that the globular Tesla field was no more than fifteen feet or so from the road. The globe goes well out of the picture frame, showing it to be quite large. The curved edge shows what looks like two portals seen at edge.

To the right of the globe are veils with different patterns in them. Some are in a round, swirling pattern; others are in sheets (indicating different types of energy?).

**4. TESLA GLOBES WITH "PLANE."** *Taken:* August 1988 at Pine Bush, New York. *Camera:* Nikon 35mm SLR with 50mm lens. *Film:* Kodacolor negative print film (ASA 400). *Exposure:* 1/60 sec. at f/1.4 with flash.

One night a group of us stood on a road and watched what we thought might be an airplane come toward us. It turned directly at us and passed overhead at an altitude of perhaps five hundred feet, with very little noise. As it came toward us, I took this flash picture.

What I got on film startled me because what we saw could easily pass for a plane. The bright lights seen here are heading directly at me. Around the object in a square formation in the sky are three medium-sized Tesla globes. The ones to the left and right of the object have deep, craterlike openings. The one at the bottom is a typical globular Tesla field. No strong image is at the left bottom corner.

A number of faintly seen Tesla fields are lined up filling out part of a four-sided image. Some of them almost look like reflections of the strong-imaged Tesla field. If so, they were very close to the camera, and the camera flash through the filter caused a double image. But I am only guessing.

**5. BEAM OF LIGHT.** *Taken:* October 25, 1987 at Pine Bush, New York. *Camera:* Nikon 35mm SLR with 50mm lens. *Film:* Kodacolor negative print film (ASA 400). *Exposure:* 1/60 sec. at f/1.4 with flash.

This is the first of several photos of beams of light. A barbed wire fence and post are at the bottom of the photo. But the beam of light is not part of the physical situation; no poles of this kind are anywhere along the roadside. Several colleagues also have gotten beams of light in photos taken in the same situation. We started getting these around mid-1987.

**6.** FORMATION OF LIGHTS. *Taken:* April 1987 at Pine Bush, New York. *Camera:* Nikon 35mm SLR with 50mm lens. *Film:* Kodacolor negative print film (ASA 400). *Exposure:* 1/60 sec. at f/1.4 with flash.

I did not see anything except some flashing lights when I took this photo. It appears that individual lights from whatever type of craft this is show up in other, earlier photos, here and there, like one of the small red triangular pieces of light at the left side of the lights shown here.

The bottom row of tiny red lights are equidistant from each other. The next higher row has a slightly larger group of red dots, with larger white ones, plus the peculiar red-orange triangle pinhead-sized lights.

Their closeness to us and to the ground is startling. We find it hard to believe something like this could fly so close without our consciously hearing or seeing it, but we all seem to feel their presence physiologically, to one degree or another. We use this feeling to tell us where to aim our cameras.

**7.** LARGE TESLA FIELD. *Taken:* June 12, 1988 at Pine Bush, New York. *Camera:* Nikon 35mm SLR with 50mm lens. *Film:* Kodacolor negative print film (ASA 400). *Exposure:* 1/60 sec. at f/1.4 with flash.

At the time this photo was taken, about eight of us were in the field, with many lights in the sky. Although the Tesla field shown here wasn't visible, we must have seen a large light coming over the farm field. When I took this picture, Cindy Golas also took one with her zoom lens and got the Tesla field up close. This mutual photographic corroboration is proof that the Tesla fields are not artifacts of our cameras. I estimate the size of this Tesla field at about one hundred feet in diameter. There is also a small, round globe in the trees to the right, where the partially-hidden farther trees form a background about halfway up the tree in the foreground.

**8.** WANAQUE RESERVOIR. *Taken:* February 1981 at Wanaque Reservoir, New Jersey. *Camera:* Russian Zenite 35mm SLR with 50mm lens. *Film:* Kodacolor negative print film (ASA 400). *Exposure:* five-minute time exposure.

As described in chapter 7, we saw lights come over the small hills on the far side of the Wanaque Reservoir and move toward us. The craft was partially lit and stopped a few feet over the frozen reservoir with no sound, about one hundred feet from us. It looked small—perhaps twenty feet long—and narrow, but we couldn't tell its exact shape. We could see wires that extended from the craft bobbing as it moved.

I took several photos and this single time exposure, which doesn't show the craft or its position the way we saw it. The craft was clearly a few feet above the ice, not high in the sky, so something was spewing this chunk of light. It appears similar to the spray of light in which the aliens at Pine Bush in photo 24 are standing. After about twenty minutes, the craft turned off its lights and was lost to our sight.

**9.** TESLA AND TELEPHONE POLE. *Taken:* July 1987 at Pine Bush, New York. *Camera:* Nikon 35mm SLR with 50mm lens. *Film:* Kodacolor negative print film (ASA 400). *Exposure:* 1/60 sec. at f/1.4 with flash.

It wasn't even dark and many lights were flying. All we saw were odd-shaped lights when I took this picture. The argument is whether this Tesla globe is in front of or behind the pole.

**10.** GROUP OF LIGHTS. *Taken:* January 1985 at Pine Bush, New York. *Camera:* Nikon 35mm SLR with 50mm lens. *Film:* Kodacolor negative print film (ASA 400). *Exposure:* 1/60 sec. at f/1.4 with flash.

All we saw was an object with normal-looking strobe lights coming by flashing.

**11.** SCATTERED TESLAS. *Taken:* June 14, 1988 at Pine Bush, New York. *Camera:* Nikon 35mm SLR with 50mm lens. *Film:* Kodacolor negative print film (ASA 400). *Ex-*

*posure:* ¹⁄₆₀ sec. at f/1.4 with flash.

There were lights all over the sky, and that whole time period was extremely active for sightings and pictures. This shows a combination of opaque and near transparent Teslas as well as the globe- and football-shaped ones.

**12.** CRAFT WITH ANGLED RAYS AND SMALL GLOBE ON GROUND. *Taken:* July 1986 at Pine Bush, New York. *Camera:* Nikon 35mm SLR with 50mm lens. *Film:* Kodacolor negative print film (ASA 400). *Exposure:* ¹⁄₆₀ sec. at f/1.4 with flash.

We watched an object come directly at us and I snapped the picture. The angled ray of light is interesting, but the globe sitting on the ground under where the object passed is incredible, since it just shouldn't be there. This photo also resembles almost exactly a photo I took a month before, except those angled rays were blue and there was also a globe on the ground that the object apparently flew over. During many observations of flying objects, we realized they were flying over land on which something unusual was going on at the same time. This is why I feel the flash is so important since it seems to hit on things that shouldn't really be there.

**13.** FORMATION OF OBJECTS. *Taken:* October 1981 at Bergen County, New Jersey. *Camera:* Nikon 35mm SLR with 50mm lens. *Film:* Kodacolor negative print film (ASA 400). Five-minute time exposure, 10:00 P.M. (star trails in photo).

For several months, my family and neighbors were seeing UFOs at least once a week over our New Jersey homes. One night we realized that after the regular air traffic had stopped, there were a number of objects continually circling the area. I decided to set my camera on a tripod and take some time exposures. There were enough objects to have me go through a 24-frame roll. This picture is 24B—in other words, this roll of film had an extra frame and it was the only picture that showed something significant.

**14.** LARGE TESLA GLOBE. *Taken:* July 1989 at Pine Bush, New York. *Camera:* Nikon 35mm SLR with 50mm lens. *Film:* Kodacolor negative print film (ASA 400). *Exposure:* ⅟₆₀ sec. at f/1.4 with flash.

This was another one of those nights when plenty of lights were flying around and we snapped away, knowing from past experience the chances were good we would get on film much more than we saw. It's very unnerving to look at a photo after the fact and see something this big, dead center in the picture, realizing it was right there and we couldn't see it—but obviously we could feel the presence.

**15.** TWO PAIRS OF DUAL LIGHTS. *Taken:* February 21, 1990. Middletown, New York. *Camera:* Nikon 35mm SLR with 50mm lens. *Film:* Kodacolor negative print film (ASA 400). *Exposure:* ⅟₆₀ sec. at f/1.4 with flash. Series of eight.

I was driving back into Middletown to the highway to go home when I suddenly realized an object was paralleling me to my right over the fields. I slowed up and I realized the lights were every which way on it. I pulled over. The large object made a sharp turn-around and came back towards me. I snapped off a number of pictures as the thing passed over me. At the close distance I was to it, I still wasn't sure of the shape. This first picture of the series is the only one with a second set of lights above the bright squarish dual lights.

In looking through my other pictures from the last few years, I found photos of what appears to be the same object, with the squarish dual headlights and a second set of dim lights above it. This might indicate either the two objects always fly together, are attached, or the construction of the front of the craft has height to it.

**16.** TRIANGLE CRAFT AND EMANATIONS. *Taken:* July 18, 1980 at Pine Bush, New York. *Camera:* Russian Zenite 35mm SLR with 50mm lens. *Film:* Kodacolor negative print film (ASA 400). *Exposure:* ⅟₆₀ sec. at f/2.0.

This triangle craft was hovering above us at a height of several dozen feet—not much higher than the utility poles along the road. This view looks upward at the underside of the craft, which is partially surrounded by the alternating current on the right side of the frame. All emissions were unseen.

The right edge of the craft is visible if the darkness of the print is varied. The emissions surround the viewer's left edge of the craft and the underside. They appear to be shooting from a vent in the front and side of the craft. Details of the emissions show what looks like an alternating current running through the center of the discharge. The edges of the discharge appear gold and reddish in color.

In the center of the horizontal discharge is a bluish cloud—ultraviolet radiation again. This seems to appear somewhere in most photographs of UFOs.

**17.** TRIANGLE CRAFT WITH EMANATIONS. *Taken:* July 1980 at Pine Bush, New York. *Camera:* Nikon 35mm SLR with 50mm lens. *Film:* Kodacolor negative print film (ASA 400). *Exposure:* $\frac{1}{60}$ sec. at f/1.4. Series of nine.

This was taken the first night in Pine Bush from the initial series of photos. The triangle ships hovered over us and I took this head-on shot of the clear-cut craft. The front of the craft has large windows and a bowed plus-sign lighting panel separating each of the four windows. For this discharge to cover the craft thoroughly, it would have to come out of vents around the windows, or the lighting system itself may be giving off the discharge around the whole ship, which would explain why we can't photograph what we see clearly.

The bluish blur around the white portion of the discharge is a "textbook symptom" of how ultraviolet radiation photographs. The blue portion appears to engulf the rest of the triangle craft—the body, and the legs of the triangle, which comes to pointed ends.

**18.** TWO ALIENS. *Taken:* July 18, 1980 at Pine Bush, New York. *Camera:* Russian Zenite 35mm SLR with

50mm lens. *Film:* Kodacolor negative print film (ASA 400). *Exposure:* ⅟₆₀ sec. at f/2.0.

What we saw were 10 to 20 triangle craft with various flashing lights on them in assorted colors. Some craft were above us and some were sitting on the ground or landing. All were silent. They were as close as 50 feet to several hundred feet away when the photos were taken. We later matched up pod marks, indicating the triangle ships were about 60 feet on each side or 180 feet in perimeter.

This craft was on the ground, and what we saw was its flashing lights at ground level. High, thick foliage prevented us from approaching it.

Two figures stand on either side of a dome-shaped object, which I believe is the back of the triangle craft. The craft slopes downward into a hump or dome, tapering off at the back end.

The figure on the left has a segmented-looking body and misshapen arms with a dark covering where hair should be. The figure on the right wears what appears to be a cab driver's cap (a souvenir?). Details of the face and body are shadowed, but a hint of a face shows something is really there and looking toward the camera. (Betty Hill said under hypnosis that when she was abducted with her husband Barney, in 1961, one of the aliens wore a "cabby's" cap, and that cap is depicted in some of her illustrations.)

In the immediate sky area above the bottom dome and figures are three discharges or emanations, which were not seen by our eyes, but were picked up on film. From the other photographs it appears the ships have vents and use them to release these emissions. In this case, the vent would be on top of the craft and the emissions would be sprayed upward, as this photograph shows. These emissions are examples of "chunks" of light.

**19.** FIVE ALIENS. *Taken:* July 18, 1980 at Pine Bush, New York. *Camera:* Russian Zenite 35mm SLR with 50mm lens. *Film:* Kodacolor negative print film (ASA 400). *Exposure:* ⅟₆₀ sec. at f/2.0.

What we saw were triangle craft, as described above. This photo probably shows the same craft as in the photo of the two aliens. As noted, foliage prevented our getting closer. This craft is using different emanations which, again, our eyes did not observe. Whether the craft moved or turned within the few minutes between the time I took this photo and the preceding one is unknown to me because of the momentary excitement. We did shift our position a few feet to the side during that time.

Four figures stand at the base of a spray of unseen clumps of light on the right side of the frame. A pair of lights on the left of the frame were also unseen. Both light sources give off light and reflect onto the unlit structure of the craft, which can be vaguely seen lying horizontally along the ground with portions perpendicular to the ground, indicating a full structure is present.

At about center, between the right spray and left pair of lights, a long, thin right arm with hand and thumb can be seen. This figure—Number 5 in the tracing—is looking downward and wore the cap, which is why it looks like the figure from the photo of the two aliens. It seems to be walking into an entrance to the craft, whose color appears to be amber, possibly due to lighting.

Each of the five figures appears to be totally different in form. As the tracing shows, Number 1 wears a dark head covering and a dark, ankle-length robe. The left arm is bent and appears to be sectioned, coming to a point, not a hand. There are rabbit-ear antennae on the head, making this figure look robotic rather than biological. It is facing Number 2 and Number 3; there is a hint of the left side of a "flesh-toned" face.

Number 2 has its back to the camera and is looking at Number 3. Number 2 also appears robotic with rabbit-ear antennae on something pointed (the head or something on the head). This figure seems to wear a white or light-colored dresslike garment, coming to about the knees, with dark pants legs showing on the shin. The shading and shadows of Number 2 and Number 3 indicate the light source to be the white spray in back of them, which also shows the figures are definitely three-dimensional.

The left arm of Number 2 is outstretched to the right arm of Number 3, who is facing Number 2. Number 3 appears to be conversing with Number 2, who wears a long, draped sleeve on a white or light-colored tunic top, with dark pants. This alien looks stocky and hairless with very dark eyes, only the left of which can be seen as a dot, suggesting the eye is completely black.

Number 3 looks like the alien named Quaazga whom Betty Andreasson says she saw in her encounter in *The Andreasson Affair*.

Number 4 appears to stand away from the other three, closer to the camera, making it look taller. A large clump of spray covers its face, so no details can be seen. This thin figure seems to wear a dark jumpsuit with baggy legs. The jumpsuit has a waist and lowcut V-neck. A flesh-colored neckline where the V-neck is can be seen.

The bluish cloud of light behind the white spray is ultraviolet radiation, according to the explanation, found in any physics textbook, of how ultraviolet light photographs. The white spray is also characteristic of photographic effects from fusion power. I suspect fusion powers the ships.

# CHAPTER 17

• • •

# FRONTIERS OF SCIENCE

I RECOGNIZED WHEN I recruited people to come with me to Pine Bush that each night's events would probably vary from the others. I also recognized that the ships seemed to have varied reactions to the people with me. Some people seemed to be extremely conducive to close-range sightings every time they came along—which is, of course, precisely what I wanted. Other people saw only distant lights doing weird things in the sky for hours on end. Still other people saw nothing. A fourth group—extremely small—saw aliens, either on the ground or through an abduction experience. (I know of several people in the Pine Bush area who either remember seeing aliens or have told me of their "missing time" experiences, in which they apparently were abducted by aliens.)

All of us, whatever the category, had the same "big" questions about UFOs, and none have been answered adequately. Here are clusters of things we want to know.

1. What are UFOs? Where do they come from? Why are they here?
2. Why have they come essentially in secret? Why have they traveled to earth if they are from another solar system? Why are they camouflaging them-

selves? Are the aliens doing something we would consider wrong?

3. Why has their contact with humans been so limited and confusing? Why have some people who had contact with them been persecuted?

4. Why is the United States government, and other governments, so secretive about UFOs?

5. Are what we call psychic or paranormal abilities involved with aliens and ships? Are ships using something that disturbs a "doorway" that permits psychic events (what I call fringe experiences) to occur?

6. What are the ships doing that requires them to land night after night in the same areas? (Pine Bush is one of hundreds of "hot" areas.)

We are far from having indisputable answers, but here is a summary of the data collected so far by me and my colleagues, and our collective insights. The data, consisting of personal experiences by several dozen people, plus photographs by half a dozen witnesses, are consistent and lead to recognizable patterns.

*1. About fifteen different but nonetheless standard craft shapes have been seen* around the world—triangle, diamond, rectangle, boomerang, and octagon—along with various hybrid shapes altered through external attachments and appendages, such as antennaelike devices. Lights on some of the craft are rounded and detached from the ship's body, leading people to think the craft is round. But classical flying saucer-shaped craft haven't been reported since 1980. The ships have relied on their lighting systems to fool people.

*2. Clear photographs of the ships aren't possible with glass-lensed cameras.* All household cameras have glass lenses. The ships release short wave radiation—ultraviolet, x-ray, and gamma ray—which our eyes don't see but which film registers. A quartz or plastic lens is needed to take clear photos of the craft under those conditions.

3. *The ships power themselves through nuclear fusion.* I grant that other systems may also be involved, such as psychotronics in the propulsion system proper to achieve antigravitation. Nevertheless, fusion is clearly indicated by my analysis. If UFOs are extraterrestrial, they need a tremendous amount of fuel or a tremendously efficient propulsion system, or both, to cross astrophysical space. Specific elements in my photographs match elements found in solar photographs, i.e., x-ray emissions. The sun runs on nuclear fusion. Photographing an artificial source of nuclear fusion would produce the same results as photographing the sun.

4. *The ships imitate planes,* sometimes with flashing strobes and an approximation of standard navigational lights, but often without any engine noise. Probably much more UFO activity is going on than the UFO research community is aware of.

5. *Certain unique conditions in the Pine Bush area seem associated with the UFOs.* The Wallkill River runs from south to north—one of only several rivers in the continental United States to do so. Also, the rare metals beryllium, titanium, and zirconium and the rare minerals franklinite and wollastonite are found in Orange County, New York, but nowhere else in North America.

6. *The ships' external covering has a quality that can render the ship invisible or transparent* unless the ship is lit. The ships' lights illuminate the portion of the ship immediately surrounding the lights. When a ship turns out all its lights, it seems to disappear as if dematerialized, but it has only vanished from our optical view, not from our space-time. I believe the ships' "skin" is at least partly metallic.

7. *The aliens seem to be watching certain people, and the national government seems to be watching the same people.* Why, I don't know.

8. *The aliens have released wildlife not indigenous to*

*the Pine Bush area.* Hunters primarily have seen out-of-place animals, such as lemurs.

9. *Construction of underground installations appears to be under way in the Pine Bush area.* Underground sounds—apparently generators, drills, and turbines—have been heard in the woods and fields at all hours of the night. We have had reports of similar noises in other parts of the country where UFO activity is occurring.

10. *The underground installations are being linked through mining systems across the country.*

11. The number of ships is too large and the level of activity too high to go unnoticed by government authorities. *We believe permission has been given by high levels of government for the aliens to proceed with their operations* without interference and without publicity.

12. *Aliens can't breathe our atmosphere for long.* Humans abducted by aliens can't breathe properly while inside a UFO and need oxygen. On many occasions aliens have been seen wearing apparatus apparently intended to help them breathe better.

13. *Aliens don't "channel" through people.* Anyone who claims to be channeling aliens is mislabeling the situation. Assuming the channeling is genuine, the source might be spirit guides, the Higher self, the subconscious—but it is not aliens.

14. People who have been abducted say that on occasion they have seen human-looking beings aboard the ships—and they obviously are not abductees because they seem to be working with the aliens. If humans are on the ships by choice, it is logical to conclude that *some humans are assisting the aliens and may be doing so on earth as well as aboard craft.* Some of those humans may hold positions of power and influence in government and other institutions in nations around the world.

The aliens have confused every aspect of the way we perceive them, so although we have made some progress towards an understanding of certain aspects of UFO phenomena, we are no closer to the ultimate answers (who they are and where they come from) today than when the modern era of UFO research began forty years ago. The aliens' imitations of aircraft lighting enables them to mix among planes in the sky day and night. The implications are staggering: it smells of "invasion."

Some nights dozens of ships seem to be in the sky; other nights there may be only a few. But they all continually go back and forth along the contour of the tree lines, circling around the same fields, dropping down, even landing, in the same spots in the fields over and over, for hours on end. The only sense I make of it is that the aliens are working on something in or on the ground, with much of their activity shielded from photographic record through the use of shortwave radiation, picked up by our film but not our eyes. Likewise, the aliens can operate through stealthy means to keep us from seeing with our eyes where they are and what they're doing.

Years ago, when I discovered there was an "invisibility" screen—for lack of a better term—I tried to outwit the aliens by driving down a road, stopping suddenly and simply running into the field, taking anyone in the car along with me. More often than not (at the height of activity, perhaps 80 to 90 percent of the time), a ship was sitting in the field; our spontaneous approach forced it to take off to avoid contact. We achieved some of our best sightings this way. But apparently the aliens decided not to land in the front fields near roads if I was going to run into them. Instead, they now land on the inner fields beyond the treelines and are therefore relatively inaccessible.

The behavior patterns of the aliens in their ships and their continuous interaction with people leave me and my colleagues feeling violated on some level. How could we feel otherwise when confusion, manipulation, and deception are the chief forms of alien behavior? We also feel we are continuously watched—not every second of the day, but perhaps for a week or two in a row. Then the surveillance will stop for a month or so, begin again, then stop again. This happens erratically, but definite occurrences indicate the monitoring is real and not simply due to an overactive imagination.

Since the aliens appear to be running a covert operation, they probably are acting within a command structure much like a military hierarchy. If so, they must have orders to perform some activities and to refrain from others. If their activities include giving someone a close encounter of the alien kind, then that person will somehow be manipulated into a position where he or she will see an alien or be abducted by them.

Though I have known people who fought off an abduction, I'd say that in most cases if the aliens are going to get you, you can't do much about it. Budd Hopkins points out in *Intruders* that the aliens come into people's homes to do what they want. In the cases of Betty Andreasson and Whitley Strieber, their perception of the aliens is that they seemed to materialize within the house, passing through solid walls in ghostlike fashion. Every encounter and sighting seems well planned, particularly the abductions involving medical examinations. Some abductees talk about the smoothness of the operation they underwent involuntarily.

The last time I had a very close sighting—I was within touching distance of a craft—I had enough presence of mind to look around quickly at the sky to see what else was flying. The craft was a small boomerang hovering above me and my car; I saw at least two other ships in close proximity. The boomerang was so low that I couldn't lean over to turn on my tape recorder, which I had sitting on the hood of my car, because I would have hit my head on the craft and I was afraid of possible burns if I touched the craft.

Seeing the other two ships close by led me to think they probably used the buddy system and did nothing alone. My impression has since been confirmed by other close sightings because I've seen other ships lingering in the background on those occasions.

Close encounters seem to be written into the aliens' plan. So do other activities. On some nights, when the weather was perfect and I thought I had "good" people with me, the sky seemed dead. On other nights, when we were loosely organized and not well prepared for anything, the most incredible sightings would occur. And in between those extremes have been plenty of interesting experiences when we got some degree of what we came for. We don't know why some people see UFOs constantly and others never see them, and still others desperately want to see them but don't.

The last thing I want to discuss is the notion that the UFOs reported in the Hudson Valley area—including what I've reported here—are sightings of the B-2 Stealth bomber. The Stealth bomber has a boomerang shape similar to the *Westchester Wing* so some people conclude it has a double identity. According to a February 2, 1989 story on page twelve in the [Albany, New York] *Times Union,* Mark Rodeghier of the Center for UFO Studies in Evanston, Illinois, said, "It looks very curious that while the Stealth bomber was under development, beginning in 1981, this boomerang object, that looks remarkably like the bomber in profile and could not be spotted on radar, was being sighted continually. And then, even more interesting, is that the sightings suddenly evaporated just before the plane was unveiled."

Philip Imbrogno, who kindly wrote the Foreword to this book, doesn't dismiss the possibility completely either. He told Paul Grondahl, the reporter who wrote the *Times Union* story, "It's something to be considered," adding that he found "no facilities and no suggestions that the Stealth bomber was ever [in Westchester, New York]."

The article points out that experimental aircraft are simply not test-flown over populated areas such as Westchester. Also, witnesses of the Westchester UFO reported that it hovered noiselessly at very low altitudes, something the Stealth bomber would not be capable of doing.

I agree with Imbrogno that the B-2 Stealth bomber unveiled in late 1988 is not what my colleagues and I have been seeing in Pine Bush. I have no doubt whatsoever about the nonhuman origin of those craft. My certainty is based on seeing aliens and photographing them several times in proximity to their craft.

However, this situation may have a strange twist. I believe there may be forms of Stealth aircraft that are *true* UFOs built and operated by human beings. The military/ intelligence people behind these aircraft, whose shapes include some similar to the B-2, would have built them with assistance from the aliens. If a longstanding contact has existed between our government and an alien civilization, as several ufologists have claimed and as my own findings suggest, technology transfers may have occurred from them to us, in return for whatever they might have wanted from us. Most likely they wanted permission to conduct their scientific examinations of people whom they abduct, or at least they wanted a promise of noninterference by our government. It looks as if they got what they wanted, at the expense of the civil and human rights of unfortunate American citizens who have been abducted by aliens. And following the logic of this proposition, it also then looks as if the B-2 Stealth bomber shown to the public is really a decoy to divert attention from where the money and effort are really being placed—namely, on construction of enhanced stealth craft capable of hovering at ground level, cruising at speeds ranging from a slow walk to thousands of miles per hour, and turning invisible to the human eye. In other words, American UFOs.

I am drawing upon the assertions and speculations of UFO investigators whose work led them in this direction and who have commented about it publicly. It makes sense to me, given my personal experience, to come to this conclusion from their data. I have no proof of it, and I am not asserting it as fact. I am only offering it for consideration. But it could mean there *is* a kind of double identity to the Stealth bomber, although not the straightforward one suggested in the *Times Union* article. The implications for the security of the United States are appalling, however. It means the silent invasion is proceeding with the help of a fifth column of quislings and traitors who have sold the national birthright of their fellow citizens for rewards that can only be guessed at. It would be an invisible government at its worst.

So where are those of us who have had close encounters with aliens from another world? We are a few steps closer to the truth, yet, the more we know, the feeling becomes more and more perplexed and frustrated. Each new data point, each new answer, raises a dozen new questions— some biological, some sociopolitical, some parapsychological, some metaphysical. Scientific and spiritual dimensions converge in the study of the UFO phenomenon, but mainstream scientists, such as those at NASA and the Planetary Society, avoid the subject, as do mainstream religious and spiritual institutions. Funding and resources are scarce for serious but unaffiliated researchers. We work on the fringes of official science and are seen as the lunatic fringe, at that, by closed-minded people with preconceived views of how the universe should be.

My colleagues and I want answers to a cosmic puzzle. We have some pieces that fit, but many more are needed before the pattern is absolutely clear. We need more people to take active roles in research by direct observation, with technical resources far beyond what we've been able to employ thus far. People need to look up. UFOs are seen not just in isolated places. The more who see what is occurring, the better off we'll be.

Aliens are on our planet. They haven't come in the manner popularly hoped for. They've come covertly, invading in silence. The sooner we find out why they are here, the sooner we will answer our questions and the sooner we will know whether humanity should brace itself for the beginning of the end—or the end of the beginning.

# APPENDIX

**• • •**

# EYEWITNESS STATEMENTS

## STATEMENT BY ELEANOR MOTICHKA OF WAYNE, NEW JERSEY

We were on a side road [in Pine Bush on Sunday, October 21, 1984 about ten o'clock P.M.] and decided to walk into a large field there. There was a low-lying fog in the field. Ellen pulled over and we crawled under a barbed wire fence. Ellen left her tape recorder and flashlight in the car. We didn't take ten steps when dual headlights lifted off the back corner of the field, maybe six hundred feet from us, and came toward us. The craft came to about mid-field and turned to move across the field going north (to our left).

The rectangle shape was completely lit up with seams in the metal. It had a flat back with a tiny red light hanging from a wire like a wagging tail. Four yellow lights were in each corner of the belly of the craft, which may have been thirty feet off the ground, if that. The craft looked about the size of the triangle craft we normally had seen, or a little bigger.

It was going about five miles per hour and sounded like a Boeing 747. It got to the north end of the field (moving a total of about five hundred feet across the field) and turned *off* the noise but kept moving slowly, going over the road. It stopped dead, turned toward us, and shut out all the lights and we couldn't see it anymore.

(This was the same night we later saw the lemur.)

## STATEMENT BY CATHY MCCARTNEY OF BERGENFIELD, NEW JERSEY

1. Observed one evening was a ship of the kind Ellen dubs the "jumbo jet." We chased it one night in Bob Lloyd's pickup truck. After several minutes of the ship dodging our maneuvers, we felt we had a decent view of it and parked the truck. Jumping out of our vehicle, we found that the ship, too, had stopped, but only momentarily, and certainly *not* to pose for our cameras. The object virtually immediately took off in the opposite direction, *without turning its nose around*. As it flew away backward, my amazement left me only able to stare. "Ellen," I said after it had gone, "did you see that?" "Yes," she replied, "they do things like that."

2. I was witness to a daylight sighting late one afternoon while Ellen and I were driving through Pine Bush. A large bright red rectangular craft hovered silently over the treetops. Ellen, who was at the wheel, also saw it. The object was only in view for about two seconds. We saw no trace of it for the rest of the evening.

3. Early one morning about two o'clock, Ellen and I were followed from Orange County, New York to Oradell, New Jersey by what initially was a huge yellow light. After leaving the highway the light changed making the craft visible. Because I was in the passenger seat, I saw the craft first. Two blazing yellow lights careened toward us, fairly low to the ground, angling upward to clear a house. The two lights, which we soon realized to be the wing lights of a ship, were seesawing as the craft flew so recklessly. After she pulled over, the ship pinpointed us and came to a dead halt about thirty feet above our heads. Flashing on all of its lights, we were flooded in beams. The ship was tiny,

with a black body and silver wings. It hovered over us, making no noise for about five seconds before shooting off at an amazing speed. Like the jumbo jet ship, it did not reposition its body before veering away. Wing first, the ship put itself in motion, and then after the object was already in rapid flight, it wheeled its nose around into a forward direction. At this moment, it turned off all of its lights.

I feel that this situation is highly significant because it proves that the aliens are capable of tracking and finding certain individuals. It also shows once again that the ships camouflage their true identity in the guise of earthling plane lights.

Also, by turning off their lights, they are completely undetectable by the average citizen.

4. Ellen and I were viewing a ship from the cemetery one night. It sat over a cornfield in the distance with a continual light pattern of orange-green-red-yellow. We joked that it was probably just a distraction. We ignored strange vertical clouds to the left of the UFO until they themselves began to move. Swaying back and forth, they then compressed themselves into little orbs and these cloudlike orbs then began to swirl in circles. Within each orb we observed a pulsation of light that was fogged because of the cloud that encompassed it. We watched for quite a while before they fell back to the ground. Photos revealed a white and green light within each orb.

## STATEMENT BY EDWARD MORÉT OF NEW HAVEN, CONNECTICUT

(Transcribed from an audiotape made during an August 30, 1986 sighting at Pine Bush. Also present were Ellen Crystall, Donna Sommers, and Donna Morét. They were discussing the terrain when a brilliant light appeared at a distance estimated at half a mile. The light at first was red, then got so bright that it seemed white. The total time of the sighting was about five minutes.)

Morét: . . . so what you're saying is . . . Oooh, oooh, my God! What is that? Oh, my God! Oh, my God! That is incredible! Wow!

Crystall: That was like an acknowledgment. Now, that's not Jupiter!

Morét: I know it! That ain't Jupiter. No way.

Crystall: There's another one over the trees down there.

Morét: That one is spectacular! That is incredible. I can't believe this. I can't believe this. This is incredible. [Speaking for the record] The one we're spotting right now is spectacular. Oh, my God! There's another one. There's two huge ships out here! They're phenomenal in size! I can't believe the sensation I'm getting. . . . They are massive. I have never seen anything like this. It's hard to describe. They're ships. They're very powerful. They're massive and their light—brilliant, extremely brilliant. Oh, my God, this is exciting! It seems as if they just came out. This is incredible. I can't believe this. It's something else. It's extremely bright. That was phenomenal. Where they just pulled [i.e., seemed to appear] out. They just pulled out of nowhere. They're so bright.

## STATEMENT BY CINDY GOLAS OF BEACON, NEW YORK

On Thursday, August 20, 1987, at approximately 10:15 P.M., we observed a white object in the sky just above the tree line [in Pine Bush, New York]. It started traveling down the tree line at a very slow rate of speed and at times it seemed to stop altogether. Then it seemed to rotate and head in our direction. Now there were four white lights across the front of it and they were quite a bit larger than it first appeared. We were watching it head toward us when

suddenly the end light broke away and started to fly around
the area. When it broke away, it turned red in color. The
white lights came toward us a little bit more and then
stopped and seemed to rotate. The lights turned red, and
there were only two of them. They started to fly away, and
they were at a cockeyed angle. From the time we started
watching the light until it went out of sight took a total of
thirty to forty five minutes.

## STATEMENT BY JOHN W. WHITE OF CHESHIRE, CONNECTICUT

In April 1987 I drove from my Connecticut home to Pine
Bush, New York, to meet with Ellen Crystall for a ''UFO
hunt.'' I'd been there with her three times since the beginning of the year but had seen nothing I felt could not be
explained in conventional terms—primarily as aircraft,
even though Ellen said they were UFOs disguised as aircraft. There were plenty of real aircraft, she agreed, but
what was the explanation of aircraft flying around in circles
for hours on end above Pine Bush on a Saturday night when
the local Orange County Airport was unmanned and for all
intents and purposes closed?

A good question, but I was unconvinced. As a former
naval officer with naval air training, plus my informal training as an investigator of paranormal phenomena, including
UFOs, I needed stronger evidence.

I got it on my fourth visit to Pine Bush. I was accompanied by my neighbor, Raymond Sharp, who has a master's degree in physics; my son, Tom, an electrical engineer
recently graduated from Rochester Polytechnical Institute;
his friend, Steve Staton, also a Rochester Polytechnical Institute engineer; and a married couple, Mike and Terrie
Jones, also Rochester Polytechnical Institute graduates and
friends of my son. All of them witnessed the following
event.

About ten o'clock P.M. on a bright, clear mid-April evening with a full moon overhead, we were standing beside our cars on West Searsville Road, looking eastward toward a line of trees about a quarter of a mile away which ran along the far edge of the farm field next to us. We'd seen many aircraft that night, but as we scanned the sky, we saw something different. A brilliant red light rose slowly from behind the tree line and hovered slightly above the trees. Its appearance lasted no longer than perhaps fifteen seconds before it sank below the trees again and was lost to sight. It happened so quickly that none of us had time to make any rough angular measurements of its length or height.

I'm sure the light was not an aircraft navigational light. It was rectangular, with its length about twice as long as its height. As it hovered, it suddenly changed its shape along its long axis, as if unlighted sections similar in size to the light were turned on at either end. Briefly, the red light increased to perhaps three times its length, although the light didn't expand and collapse as if it had gotten brighter. The red color remained as the same hue and intensity; it simply seemed to have additional sections lighted, instantly giving the appearance of a single, larger light. Then the end sections turned off and the light returned to its original dimensions. A few seconds later, it dropped out of sight behind the tree line.

I had been watching it through seven-power binoculars. I wear glasses for distant vision, such as when I drive or watch a movie; I had my glasses on and the binoculars adjusted for sharp focus on a distant farmhouse light. When I first saw the red light, I did the usual thing: I lowered the binoculars and blinked my eyes to determine whether something was ocularly or optically wrong. Everything was working well. I immediately raised the binoculars and resumed my observation.

During this brief time, of course, we were talking loudly to each other about the light, but merely to direct everyone's attention to it. When it disappeared, I asked everyone to describe what they'd just seen. I didn't describe my own perceptions; I wanted to validate them without biasing the witnesses. All agreed on the characteristics of what we'd observed.

What *had* we seen? I don't know. I can call it a UFO because it was an unidentified noctural light and an unidentified aerial phenomenon. I didn't see a Martian license plate on it; I didn't see a solid object with riveted seams, landing gear and antennas. But in the absence of a persuasive explanation along naturalistic lines, such as an atmospheric phenomenon or reflection of a distant light source— neither of which I consider to be remotely applicable—I'm left with an experience that is by definition a UFO sighting.


## STATEMENT BY JEFFREY MEYERS OF BRIDGEPORT, CONNECTICUT

On the evening of October 9, 1987, an acquaintance and I drove to Pine Bush, New York, where we met Ellen Crystall and several other people who had come up with her. We met them on the side of a road in the middle of farm country as Ms. Crystall had instructed. On one side of the road was a field that elevated into a series of sharp, rocky crevices while the other side of the road was a huge open field bordered by dense woods about a football field-and-a-half's length from us. There was a farmhouse about one hundred yards from where we were standing, obviously occupied as indicated by the lights inside the house. There were two other farmhouses about one hundred and seventy-five yards in the other direction. It was a very cold night of the full moon in October.

As we got out of the car we were greeted by Ms. Crystall. A few minutes passed and Ms. Crystall pointed out what she said was a ship in the far distance. Upon first inspection I thought to myself that the light she was pointing at could be absolutely anything until a member of the group was kind enough to lend me an extra pair of field binoculars. Through the binoculars the light could clearly be seen as highly erratic, zig-zagging within a circular pattern. "Interesting phenomenon," I thought, though skeptical that what I was seeing were possibly spacecrafts from other planets.

Suddenly a number of dogs in the area began whimpering loudly. Several minutes later what appeared to be a Cessna-type aircraft flew slowly over the tree line. The group became excited as Ms. Crystall indicated that this was one of the ships. At this point my thoughts were, "Well, these people are just another group of harmlessly misled people looking to fulfill some deep void in their lives by presupposing that private planes are UFOs."

There is a private airport nearby [Orange County Airport]. I watched as the "Cessna" flew across the field in a southeasterly direction, slightly desiring to kick myself to have wasted a Friday night, but at the same time content that what I was seeing was a private aircraft. Moments after that, though, I watched as the "Cessna" maneuvered in a manner I never ascribed to the movements of small, private planes. The plane literally stopped in midair and made a precise U-turn. It was now to the left of where we were all standing.

Perhaps a quarter mile down range visible through the trees next to the farmhouse near where we were located, at this point it headed noiselessly towards us, still maintaining its altitude. At a distance of about a football field's length at an altitude of an estimated fifteen hundred feet, the craft stopped. Looking through the binoculars I clearly saw that what appeared as one red light and one green light were now three lights blinking red, green, and blue in sequence. The intensity of the light was astounding. Though I could not make out a tangible shape to the craft, it was still for perhaps a minute. Then it began to move again, silently across the field in the direction that it had come.

The craft was about to cross the path of the full moon

where I, still skeptical, fully expected to see the shadow of some known type of aircraft. What I and those with me saw could be described as a transparent triangular-shaped object unlike anything I have ever seen before. The craft headed in a southwesterly direction, where it disappeared below the tree line on a hill about a mile away.

We got into our cars and followed. Ms. Crystall went to another field not far away in order to catch another glimpse, but to no avail. After traveling to a third field, where we saw nothing, we returned to the first site where, after about fifteen minutes of empty sky, we watched a watermelon-shaped object with a ring of light around it appear over the tree line in the distance and ascend silently into the sky, only to disappear.

We left Pine Bush that evening convinced that our experience had been of an unearthly nature, though I would hesitate to try and prove this. I am quite sure of the physical reality of what I witnessed. Friends have suggested that what I saw could possibly be part of some military project, but what would be the point of testing something top secret over a moderately populated area? The question of what I saw with my own eyes will probably never be completely resolved in my mind.

## STATEMENT BY ARLENE CLIFFORD OF ORANGE, CONNECTICUT

[This is excerpted from a letter to Ellen Crystall.]

We did enjoy the watch for the UFOs on Friday night, October 9th [1987]. We enjoyed seeing the lights. We stayed and went back on Saturday night. We parked the camper and it was very dark and quiet.

An object all lit up came over and they put a spotlight on us. The picture Lynne took on Friday night shows a few lights. . . . Took more Saturday night but did not get anything. . . .

We feel they zapped our film Saturday night. Got nothing on our still pictures.

## STATEMENT BY RENEE PETRELLA OF WAYNE, NEW JERSEY

On May 29, 1988 [in Pine Bush] lights moved in the sky like nothing I have ever seen before, treetop high, no noise. Riding down a road, five of us in one car following Ellen and Luann [her sister—see the following statement], bright lights made us stop the car and look. There were two large lights—one red and the other blue-green—through two trees. Backing up the car to get a better view, the lights were gone. We all sat there and looked at one another, saying "Did you see that?" Then we moved up the road to where Ellen and Luann had stopped. Parked in front of a horse farm, the lights came back, no noise, would come to the trees and then turn again and again, each time getting closer. Then it was gone. Not seen any more that night. We all went for coffee before our long ride home. Each of us, with a piece of paper and pen in hand, made a drawing of what we had seen, not letting the other see till we were done. We all made the same drawing. It was a night that was talked about for a long time.

## STATEMENT BY LUANN PETRELLA OF SUSSEX, NEW JERSEY

In May 1988, we began going to Pine Bush with Ellen two to three times a week. We had many sightings there, [but] the craft seemed to keep their distance, just putting on enough lights and flying certain ways that you knew it was a ship. It was a tease; they kept us coming back.

Well, the tease ended on May 29, 1988. We spotted a ship, we watched it do the usual erratic flying and light switching. We decided to try to get closer since they wouldn't come to us. On this night, besides Renee, Ellen and I, we had four more friends with us, with two cars, Ellen and I in the first car and the rest in the second car following us. We saw the second car stop a distance behind us. Within a few minutes they were behind us again. We stopped at a horse farm. We had lost sight of the ship, but apparently the ship did not lose sight of us. The second car had stopped earlier because they had a clear view of the ship coming toward them through a clearing in the trees. At treetop level the ship made a turn where the observers could see the bottom of the ship. We were standing outside the cars at the horse farm, listening to them tell us what they had just seen. Even the skeptics in the second car now knew what we had been telling them was true. They were breathless, trying to have what they had just seen sink in. When there it was as if it had been there already with lights off, and flipped the lights on, lots of lights, bright lights, and it stayed there, treetop high, for maybe a minute with no sound coming from it, and as quickly as it was turned on, it was turned off and did not come back on that night.

## STATEMENT BY DAVID DE LIA OF CLIFFSIDE PARK, NEW JERSEY

About 10:30 P.M. [on June 30, 1988, in company with Ellen Crystall, Cindy Golas, and two other women], a large light came down the tree line, put on more lights and stopped in midair, looking like it was about one-quarter of a mile away or several large farm fields behind the immediate tree line (about eight hundred feet from us). When it occasionally flashed a right light, the light was far from what appeared to be the midsection. Ellen thought the craft was what she called the "jumbo," based on past sightings of it.

This was the third Thursday in a row the jumbo had flown and come close. It was stationary and then started to rotate a bit, still hovering. No sound was heard. I got the video camera out and Ellen and I ran into the field with the equipment. Ellen was taking pictures with her 35mm. Craft was still stationary. A few minutes went by and the craft began to turn around, rotating again, and then stopping.

I wanted to go farther into the field and to the woods. Ellen kept telling me we couldn't get there from the field we were in and insisted I take video from where we were. The craft now looked like it was slowly moving, but not by much. Lights seemed to be on two sides of it. From past sightings, Ellen thought it was a diamond, but I didn't know what shape it was because you couldn't really see it. I thought the lights indicated a rounder shape. A tiny white light on the right occasionally went on and off. The craft again changed direction. Ellen described it by saying it just "swings"—simply reverses direction without turning.

The craft then changed direction without turning, still appearing to drift, and remained relatively in the same place. We had no flashlight because of our haste. The craft stopped again and just hung. Ellen kept yelling at the craft to come over to us or put on more lights. I still wanted to get closer so we walked farther into the flat field. The craft looked like it was just over the middle fields. I thought we should drive to where the ship was.

The craft started to brighten up. The lights were as bright as a movie projector light. Ellen had seen them raise the intensity of the lights on many occasions. The implications of their power is scary, to say the least.

Little lights were flying around the jumbo. They looked like flies compared to it. A light came up behind the jumbo and another light moved under it.

We walked back to the road. Cindy said she heard the helicopter noise before we had gotten up there and she expected the big one to come by because that was the usual course of events. We got into a big discussion as to how we could get closer and we decided to drive around.

It was 11:25 P.M. We drove down the road and stopped

at the middle fields. We walked into the fields to the inner fields and promptly lost the jumbo.

## STATEMENT BY JOACHIM SCHAPPER OF RIVER EDGE, NEW JERSEY

I can think of two instances which stand out most [about my] going up to Pine Bush, New York, looking for UFOs.

The first one was as follows. We were standing in a small clearing behind the cemetery and suddenly this large triangle-shaped object flew directly overhead. It was flying very close to the treetops and didn't make a sound as it passed overhead. Each corner had a blinking light. The object was otherwise completely black and was out of sight in a matter of seconds.

The second incident was as follows. We were in the cemetery and above the tree line in the distance, lights were hovering. One of them moved first to its left across the tree line and then changed direction forward. After a few seconds it began to arc toward us in the cemetery. The light then stopped and grew brighter. It hovered for a moment and then reversed itself the same way it came. The light did not turn around, but rather simply put itself into reverse.

# ABOUT THE AUTHOR

ELLEN CRYSTALL, PH. D., has her doctorate in music composition from New York University. She graduated from Rutgers University in 1978 with a bachelor's degree in music and a minor in geology. In 1982 she earned a master's degree in Music Theory and Composition from Montclair State University.

Dr. Crystall is internationally recognized for her documentation of UFOs and her UFO photographs (now numbering more than 1500) in the Middletown, New York area. Articles about her UFO research have appeared in newspapers and magazines around the world, including the *New York Times*, *Omni*, the *Bergen Record*, and the Middletown, New York, *Times Herald Record*. Her research has also appeared over news services, such as the Copley News Service (Wireless Flash) and the AP wire which appears in thousands of newspapers worldwide. Dr. Crystall has been interviewed on hundreds of radio programs worldwide including Radio Free Europe, and has appeared on many television programs including *Larry King Live*, *The Joan Rivers Show*, *Sonja Live*, *Geraldo*, *Sightings*, and *Encounters*, to discuss her UFO research.

Dr. Crystall is founder and director of Contactee, The First Organization for Research of UFOs by Direct Observation, which publishes a quarterly newsletter of current research and findings. Contactee can be reached at 1442 Hemlock Farms, Hawley, PA 18428.

Like other residents of the strange communities of Crestone and the Baca, Christopher O'Brien was drawn to the sacred valley of Native American myth. He was soon compelled to document, in disturbing detail, the inexplicable events unfolding around him and the questions they raised:

- **What is the truth behind the nightly light show of UFOs pulsing and glowing across the sky?**
- **What are the strange rumbling noises coming from underground?**
- **What is the origin of a mysterious crystal skull found in the Baca?**
- **And most frightening of all, who is responsible for the scores of cattle left bloodless and mutilated in inhuman fashion?**

Including fascinating and sometimes frightening firsthand accounts by residents of the area, *The Mysterious Valley* reveals the story of one of the most bizarre regions on the face of the earth and its chilling implications for the rest of humanity.

# THE
# MYSTERIOUS VALLEY

## CHRISTOPHER O'BRIEN

**THE MYSTERIOUS VALLEY**
Christopher O'Brien
_____ 95883-8 $6.99 U.S./$7.99 CAN.